UNDERSTAND THE BORDERLINE PERSONALITY DISORDER

How to Communicate and Give Emotional
Support to a Person With BPD While
Maintaining Control of Their Life and
Avoiding Being Manipulated

By

Marshall Punj

The information herein is solely offered for informational purposes and is universal. The presentation of the information is without a contract or any guaranteed assurance.

The trademarks that are used are without any consent, and the publication of the trademark is without permission or backing by the trademark owner. All trademarks and brands within this book are for clarifying purposes only and are owned by the book owners themselves, not affiliated with this document.

Table of Contents

Introduction

Self-esteem, interpersonal relationships, impulsive behavior, and mood are all affected by borderline personality disorder. With an evident penchant for self-harm and suicidal thoughts, as well as a fear of rejection and abandonment, there is a pattern of fast oscillation from despair to confidence. Transient psychotic symptoms include hallucinations and delusions. It is often linked to significant impairments in social, occupational, and psychological functioning, as well as a decrease in life quality. Suicide is more common in those with a borderline personality disorder.

The severity of behavioral and emotional issues in borderline personality disorder varies. Some persons with borderline personality disorder can maintain their relationships and their jobs. The most severe types cause a tremendous deal of mental discomfort in those who have them. They have recurring crises that might include impulsive aggressiveness or self-harm. They commonly seek attention from psychiatric and acute-care emergency departments due to a high frequency of co-morbidity, such as other personality disorders. Although the fundamental management ideas mentioned in this proposal apply to anybody with borderline personality disorder, the therapy suggestions are tailored to individuals with the problem in its most severe forms.

A borderline personality disorder affects less than 1% of the population, with young people most affected. Women are more likely to attend religious services than men. A borderline personality disorder is seldom diagnosed before the age of eighteen; however, the symptoms of the disease may be seen much earlier. It shows itself in various ways, and although some individuals improve with time, others may continue to suffer from social and emotional challenges. Depression, PTSD, bipolar disease, anxiety, eating disorders, drug abuse, and alcohol abuse are linked to borderline personality disorder (the signs of which are frequently confused with a borderline personality disorder). The management of co-morbid disorders is not addressed in this guideline.

Chapter 1: History of BPD & Its Causes

1.1 bipolar disorder vs. borderline personality disorder

Bipolar disorder and borderline personality disorder may induce extreme emotional reactions, impulsive behavior, and melancholy, and the two can co-occur.

Bipolar disorder and bipolar disorder with psychosis are distinct disorders with distinct signs, symptoms, and treatment options.

- Bipolar disorder is a mood disease that predominantly affects a person's emotional state, causing moods, general functioning, and motivation to fluctuate throughout periods ranging from days to months. It is estimated that 8% of Americans are affected, making it more frequent than BPD.

- Borderline personality disorder (BPD) is a personality condition in which a person's inner perception and relationships are harmed, causing them to think and behave strangely.

- Doctors can distinguish between BPD and bipolar illness when diagnosing the two conditions by asking questions regarding mood cycling, sleep, relationships, self-harm, and mania.

1.2 History of Borderline personality disorder (BPD)

In 1938, Adolph Stern coined "borderline personality" in the United States. (The majority of extra personality disorders originated in Europe.)

Stern discovered a group of patients that "fit honestly neither into the psychoneurotic group nor into the psychotic group" and coined the word "borderline" to describe how they "bordered" on other illnesses.

Otto Kernberg used the phrase "borderline personality organization" in 1975 to describe a persistent pattern of behavior and functioning marked by dysfunction and implying a damaged (psychological) self-organization.

Symptoms and behavior linked with borderline personalities, such as a highly unstable self-image, abandonment concerns, quick mood swings, rejection, and a high propensity for suicide, may become more quietly accepted, regardless of the underlying psychological structures.

Transient psychotic signs and symptoms include hallucinations and delusions. In 1978, Gunderson and Kolb established the characteristics that now constitute borderline personality disorder (BPD), and they have since been included in modern psychiatric categories.

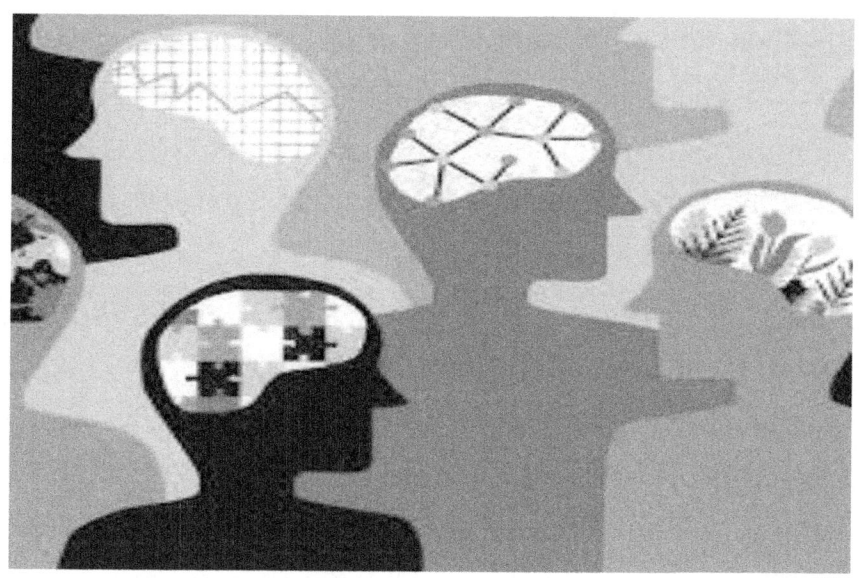

Anxiety, eating depression, and eating disorders such as PTSD, bulimia, drug addiction disorders, and bipolar disease are often co-occurring with a borderline personality disorder. Consequently, its 'borderline' status with other disorders or conceptual ambiguity (with which it is also occasionally clinically confused). There might be several connections between psychotic illnesses. People may have auditory and visual hallucinations, as well as powerful delusions, under severe conditions. Still, these are generally transitory and connected with high emotional dysfunction, distinguishing them from the basic signs and symptoms of schizophrenia and other related diseases.

Finding someone with a 'pure' BPD is rare due to the high co-morbidity. Many people believe borderline personality disorder should not be defined as a personality disorder since it overlaps with other conditions. Rather, it needs to be classified as a mood disorder or an identity issue. Some have suggested that borderline personality disorder is a kind of delayed PTSD because of its relationship to earlier trauma and resemblances to PTSD. Despite these problems, a borderline personality disorder is much more consistent than other types of personality disorders, and it is likely the most investigated. Even though some persons with borderline personality disorder come from loving and caring families, instability and relationship deprivation are more likely to encourage borderline personality rehabilitation and preventative measures.

It's critical to distinguish borderline personality disorder from "borderline intelligence," a separate concept. Individuals with severe learning disabilities, on the other hand, are more likely to have borderline personality traits (especially self-harm). A borderline personality disorder may result in a range of outcomes. Most people go through late adolescence or early adulthood; however, many may wait until later to seek psychiatric help. According to those who have undergone therapy or an official medical evaluation, at least half of those diagnosed with borderline personality disorder recover enough to no longer meet the criteria 5 to 10 years after the original diagnosis. It's unclear how much of this is due to treatment; research shows that a large portion of recovery is natural and is followed by improved self-awareness and maturity.

The age at which borderline personality disorder manifests itself is a contentious issue. Many people believe that since their personalities are still developing, they can't or shouldn't be identified in those under eighteen. Although the diagnosis is likely to be found in the Diagnostic and Statistical Manual of Mental Disorders (DSM-IV; APA, 1994), the fourth edition [DSM-IV; APA, 1994] focuses on the same principles as for adults with added caveats. Borderline signs and traits, on the other hand, may often be diagnosed considerably earlier, even before puberty. Its early manifestations in adolescent groups are increasingly gaining more attention.

Due to emotional and personal dysfunction, a borderline personality disorder is linked to considerable impairment, particularly in maintaining healthy relationships. Borderline personality disorder behaviors and symptoms are connected to various factors, including family, vocational, and social deficits. Some persons with borderline personality disorder who are also borderline in other ways may succeed at exceptionally high levels in their occupations; however, this is not always the case. Many, but not all, persons with borderline personality disorder injure themselves regularly, usually to relieve severe anguish, resulting in substantial physical injury and disability for many. Suicide is a typical occurrence among persons with borderline personality disorder, and it may happen years after symptoms first appear.

While the prognosis for borderline personality disorder is typically favorable, with most individuals failing to meet diagnostic criteria after five years, it's crucial to note that a small percentage of people may have recurrent symptoms later in life. Recurrent self-harm in the elderly may be concerning in certain situations, and the potential that it is linked to borderline personality disorder should be addressed. Unlike most other mental diseases, however, the condition is significantly less common in the elderly than in the young, and recovery is far less likely to be followed by recurrence.

Co-morbidities OF BPD

The condition of borderline personality disorder is tough to comprehend. Schizophrenia, dissociative disorders, impulsivity, depression, and other identity challenges have all been connected to BPD symptoms. This overlap is often attributed to co-morbidity, and in clinical practice, it may be difficult to discern between borderline personality disorder and other co-morbid conditions. The most significant difference between borderline personality disorder diagnostic criteria and those for other illnesses is that the symptoms of borderline personality disorder fluctuate and vary more: paranoid and psychotic symptoms are temporary, depressive symptoms and rapid change in a short period, suicidal thoughts can be intense and intolerable but only for a short time, and uncanny symptom. These signs and symptoms are much more consistent with co-morbid diseases.

Possible complications or side effects of BPD

Because they don't want to upset others, many silent BPD people fight in silence. However, if no one steps in to help, the symptoms may develop over time.

Increased the hazard of further mental disorders

This kind of borderline disorder raises your chances of having additional mental illnesses like:

- bipolar disorder
- generalized anxiety
- depression
- eating disorders
- substance abuse
- social anxiety

1.3 Causes of BPD

The specific cause of BPD, like other mental diseases, is unknown. However, there is evidence that nature (genetics or biology) and nurture (environment) are both in action. According to renowned experts, BPD is thought to arise due to environmental, biochemical, and genetic variables. It's worth mentioning, nevertheless, that the exact causes of BPD are unknown. These ideas are currently receiving support, although they are still in the early phases of development. More study is required to determine how and why the following factors are linked to BPD.

1. Environmental Causes of Borderline Personality Disorder

There is substantial evidence that BPD and stressful childhood behaviors are linked, particularly those involving caregivers. Here are a few examples of possible BPD experiences:

- Primary separation from loved ones

- Physical or emotional neglect

- Physical & sexual abuse

- Parental inattentiveness

A combination of biological features (described below) and a deceptive early environment might predispose someone to develop BPD. A child's emotional needs are not satisfied in an emotionally invalidating setting. Others who have been in a deceptive environment and those in their immediate vicinity are not always aware of their surroundings. These painful events may be suppressed or misinterpreted as praise.

These childhood incidents aren't common for people with BPD (even though a considerable number have). BPD does not emerge in every person who experiences these kinds of things. Rather than a single cause, most cases of borderline personality disorder are caused by a mix of factors.

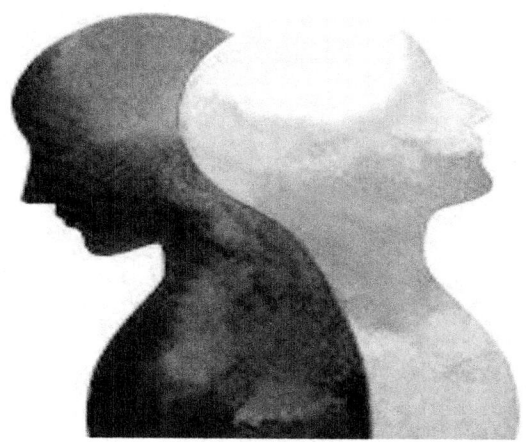

2. Biological and potential genetic causes of borderline personality disorder

Though early studies indicated that BPD did not run-in families, it was unclear if this was due to environmental factors or genetics for a long time. There is now evidence that genetic factors have a significant role in the environment. According to studies, BPD is connected to a mutation in a gene that regulates how the brain utilizes serotonin (a natural chemical present in the brain). People with this serotonin gene variant are more likely to develop BPD if they had bad childhood behaviors before (separation from caring caregivers).

According to one study, monkeys with a serotonin gene variant only exhibited symptoms that resembled BPD symptoms after being separated from their mothers and placed in less protective environments. BPD-like symptoms were considerably less likely to emerge in monkeys with the range of genes their mothers upraised. According to several studies, people with BPD have variations in the form and content of their brains. Excessive activity in brain areas that mediate emotional expression and experience has been linked to BPD. Individuals with BPD, for example, have greater levels of limbic system activity than those without the disease, which governs aggression, wrath, and fear. It might be linked to BPD's emotional insecurity symptoms. The hormone oxytocin has been linked to BPD development in recent studies.

3. Bottommost Line on Borderline Personality Disorder Cause

There's still a lot to learn about BPD's origins, and the condition is more than likely caused by a mix of factors than a single finding. As the study continues, we expect to learn more in the coming years. People who are aware of the causes of the illness are more likely to avoid contracting it, particularly if they have a biological or genetic predisposition. In the present circumstance, an invalidating environment is damaging to a child regardless of whether or not it increases the risk of BPD later on, and therapists must be aware of this condition in youngsters.

While it might be challenging to be as affirming as possible to children with biological vulnerabilities who may develop BPD, many words are praised on the surface. Feelings can easily be misinterpreted as the child's oversensitivity. Adults who were emotionally invalidated as children must learn to distinguish between invalidating and validating others' comments to avoid additional harm and improve interpersonal connections.

Characteristics that may raise the risk of BPD

- **Brain structure:** BPD patients exhibit abnormalities in brain structure and function, particularly in the brain areas that control impulses and regulate emotions. It's also unclear if BPD or other factors cause these disparities.

- **Family history:** If you have a parent or sibling, you are more likely to acquire BPD.

- **Negative experiences:** Many persons with BPD have had a difficult childhood experience, such as neglect, trauma, or child abuse, or have grown up alienated from their loved ones. However, not everyone who develops BPD, and even those who do not develop BPD, experienced one or both of these childhood behaviors.

Borderline personality disorder has several risk factors

Many factors influence the development of borderline personality disorder. Borderline personality disorder does not impact anybody who has risk factors.

- Neglect or abandonment as a kid or teenager

- As a teenager or kid, you may experience family disturbances or separations.

- Family relationships are strained.

- You may have been subjected to physical abuse as a kid or teenager.

- As a youngster or teenager, you have been sexually abused.

- Female gender

- Strained relationship with parents.

Borderline personality disorder complications

A borderline personality disorder may have serious implications if left untreated or badly managed, even life-threatening in certain cases. By following the treatment plan, you and your health care provider can reduce the chance of significant effects. A borderline personality disorder is linked to a slew of issues, including:

- Problems maintaining relations

- Eating disorders

- Abuse of alcohol or drugs

- Financial or legal problems

- Difficulties at work

- Depression

- Stressed familial relationships

- Self-harm

- Social isolation

- Suicide

Chapter 2: Symptoms & Types of BPD with their management

2.1 General Symptoms of BPD

Some indications & symptoms include:

- Depression

- Dissociative states, mainly when distressed

- Pervasive and profound moods of shame

- Uncertainty about one's goals, ambitions, career direction, or core standards

- Suicidal feelings

- Moodiness

- Hypersensitivity, particularly to perceived rejection or criticism

- A predisposition to devalue or idealize others

- Thought in terms of white and black

- Anxiety about losing power

- Difficulty with sticking or creating plans

- Anxiety, nervousness, stress, concern, and fear are all rising.

- Feelings of powerlessness and hopelessness

- Thoughts of emptiness that persist

- High self-criticism

- Unease and apprehension about the unknown

- An unstable or low self-image and self-esteem

- Risk-taking actions, like gambling and sexual promiscuity

- Separation anxiety

- Feelings that are unreasonably strong in comparison to the emotion's trigger

- Feelings that are easy to elicit

- Hostility

2.2 BPD diagnostic markers (symptoms) that are precise

The Diagnostic and Statistical Manual of Mental Disorders, Fifth Edition (DSM-5) was released by the American Psychiatric Association in 2013, and it defined nine essential diagnostic criteria (symptoms) for BPD. Five of the nine criteria must be met to diagnose the borderline disorder.

It is now standard practice to split the disease's symptoms into four categories or domains:

Domain A.

Emotional outbursts are excessive, unstable, and poorly controlled.

Depression, anger, and anxiety are the most often experienced emotions in borderline disorder. Three of the nine DSM-5 borderline disorder criteria fall under this category:

- Affective (emotional) disorder symptoms include extreme, episodic feelings, sorrow, wrath, and panic/anxiety attacks.

- Furthermore, the wrath that is unrestrained, strong, and difficult to manage

- Regularly, I get emptiness-related thoughts.

If you have the borderline disorder, you may also feel intense hyper-reactivity ("psychological storms"), an emotional reaction that is sometimes inadequate, and recurring periods of boredom and loneliness.

Domain B.

Impulsive behavior that is harmful to you or others.

This category includes two of the DSM-5 borderline disorder criteria:

Self-destructive habits are excessive spending, dangerous and improper sexual behavior, binge eating, reckless driving, and drug addiction. Suicidal ideas, gestures, attacks, or self-harming activities like hitting or cutting oneself regularly. (If you cut yourself when you're frightened, see a psychiatrist figure out why; it's a hazardous habit, and one of the most common reasons is borderline disorder.) You may also engage in more impulsive activities, such as injuring or destroying yourself, your belongings, or others.

Domain C.

Inaccurate judgments of others and yourself and increased degrees of dishonesty. This category includes two of the DSM-5 borderline disorder criteria:

- A self-image or feeling of self is visibly and repeatedly unstable (your impressions about your identity and yourself).

- Suspicion of others' opinions of you, and even delusional ideation, or stress-related dissociation periods in which you feel unreal about yourself or your surroundings.

This domain is marked by "all-or-nothing" or split thinking, difficulties "pulling" your emotions together so that they make sense, and reasonable problem resolution, particularly in social confrontations.

Domain D.

Finally, you may find yourself in relationships that are undisciplined and unstable.

This category includes the last two DSM-5 criteria:

- You may make desperate efforts to escape being abandoned, whether real or imagined.

- Your relationships may be intense and tumultuous, with you alternatively idealizing and undervaluing people close to you.

You'll also learn that you're too dependent and clingy in romantic relationships. Furthermore, you may have a high expectation of most people's negative and unhealthy attitudes and actions, as well as trouble thinking logically in challenging social settings.

2.3 Borderline personality disorder comes in a variety of forms

According to field specialist Theodore Million, there are four types of BPD:

- Self-destructive BPD
- Impulsive BPD
- Discouraged BPD
- Petulant BPD

1. Borderline personality disorder has been discouraged

Despite her unhappiness, the discouraged borderline engages in codependent and clingy behavior that she can see outside of a group setting. They are frequently filled with resentment and hostility aimed at individuals all around them under the surface.

Borderline depressed people are more prone to self-mutilate or perhaps kill themselves. They desire to be liked, yet they shun other people, feel worthless, and are prone to depression.

BPD is divided into four subtypes. BPD is one of these subtypes that should be avoided. The dependent parts of a person's personality disorder govern how they are supposed to feel and act when they have discouraged borderline.

From the outside, a person with a discouraged borderline may seem to have a determined personality disorder, according to Psychology Today. In the majority of their relationships, this individual is codependent.

When a discouraged borderline type relies on someone who does not accept dependence, such as a casual acquaintance or a new girlfriend or boyfriend, dependency is frequently obvious. When this subtype of borderline disorder is paired with one or more of the other kinds, the individual may seem severe or depressed on the outside. Clinginess and a servile "follower" mindset define the discouraged borderline.

In the worst-case situation, this individual may seem indecisive or weak-willed on the outside. They are often tormented on the inside by their lack of leadership and hatred for others around them. Self-harm, such as self-mutilation or suicide, may result from this kind of borderline disorder.

Who has this illness?

BPD and its discouraged BPD variant can affect men and women of any age, but the disease is more common in women than in men. It could be linked to a neurobiological factor, such as low estrogen levels or prejudice caused by institutionalized sexism. According to some studies, the disorder affects both men and women. Yet, women are more likely to seek therapy, be advised to seek treatment, or be formally misdiagnosed or labeled as BPD. This diagnosis is made most frequently during adolescence, and it is usually made before the age of 18. Approximately 1.6 percent of Americans will be diagnosed with BPD in any given year.

Signs Of Discouraged BPD

According to the DSM-V, BPD encompasses many signs and symptoms. When diagnosing BPD or the frustrated borderline subtype, clinicians look for the following indicators. These are defects in the formation of one's personality.

- **Impairments in self-serving.** A disordered or negative self-image, excessive self-criticism, constant feelings of emptiness, and tension-induced dissociation episodes are examples of these impairments. Inconsistencies in objectives, professional goals, values, or general expectations may be blamed.

- **Impairments in interpersonal performance.** Reduced empathy presents itself as a decreased capacity to understand others' perspectives, a dramatic and heightened perception of purported criticism or rejection, and black-and-white thinking about individuals – most people are seen as horrible or wonderful examples of these flaws. Intimacy issues might suggest a problem with interpersonal functioning. These issues may manifest as strong and dysfunctional relationships characterized by high tension, distrust, fear of rejection, clinginess, and over-participation or withdrawal at various times.

A person with borderline BPD has other traits that set them apart from the normal population. The following are some of the signs and symptoms to keep an eye out for:

- Excessive reliance and loss of independence, or fear of "inescapable" identity loss

- Hostility is a strong emotion triggered by a feeling of rejection or criticism.

- Dangerous risk-taking without regard for the consequences

- Fear of being rejected

- Uncertainty and audacity

- Anxiety over being apart

- Uncertainty and dissatisfaction

- Feelings of hopelessness or depression

- Emotions that seem to be disproportionately strong concerning the cause of an emotion

- Shame

- Fixation on negative habits from the past or those that are expected to occur in the future

- Sticking to or making plans is difficult.

- Anxiety, stress, concern, uneasiness, or panic in general

- Suicidal thoughts or actions

- Anxiety about losing control

- Impulsivity

- Moodiness

- Emotional qualities that are unstable

- Determination caused by distress

- Aroused feelings, without a doubt.

- Dissociation or "zoning out" and inability to concentrate

Some BPD symptoms that are particular to the discouraged borderline are as follows:

- Involvement in imaginary-based media and reliance on imagination to escape (movies, novels, comics, etc.)
- Because of poor self-esteem, fragility, and insecurity, he is humble.
- Abuse of drugs and alcohol
- Constant feelings of insecurity and vulnerability
- Episodes that make you cry
- Intentional loss or destruction of property, whether by physical violence against property or a cycle of acquiring, selling, or giving away property.
- Self-deprivation (as opposed to self-indulgence), founded on feelings of inadequacy
- Dependence on others to an unhealthy degree
- When it travels alongside one's demands, it is pliant and readily persuaded by others.
- Self-victimization and self-persecution; believing that others are always malicious or aggressive
- Constant ideas were jeopardized.

- Criticisms of recurring or chronic illnesses, occasionally somatic Loyalty, but only to a severe degree

- Feeling sad, powerless, helpless, and hopeless

- Even when asking a crucial role, passive and meek

- Feelings of emptiness

Causes & correlations

It's difficult to determine the exact etiology of BPD and its discouraged subtype, as it is with many mental health problems. The etiology of this sickness, according to specialists, is complicated and not readily or quickly recognizable. While BPD is difficult and encompasses a wide variety of life events, many experts in the field seem to agree on important contributing elements. The following are some of the causes and connections:

- Environmental factors such as social and familial stability are important away from trauma.

- BPD and post-traumatic stress disorder (PTSD) may be linked.

- Social aspects, including childhood social practices

- Genetics, particularly in the areas of DAT and genes DRD4 and chromosome 9

- Children's neglect and abuse, particularly sexual abuse, are common causes of childhood trauma.

- Congenital brain abnormalities, such as a smaller amygdala or hippocampus

- Estrogen concentrations, for example, neurobiological factors.

Complexity with diagnosis

BPD and its subcategories may be difficult to diagnose, even for the most experienced mental health professionals. According to research published in Scientific American in 2011, evaluating the illness is often inaccurate in some way. Women with the syndrome are more likely to have co-occurring conditions, making an accurate diagnosis challenging. Severe depression, eating disorders, anxiety disorders, antisocial personality disorder, and drug addiction are common co-morbidities with BPD. Low self-esteem or a poor self-image are common symptoms of co-occurring diseases.

Treatment of Discouraged

BPD must be monitored and treated if individuals live a productive and enjoyable life to the best of their abilities. It's particularly crucial since BPD has been linked to a higher risk of suicide. Many suicides are caused by self-harm and suicidal impulses in persons with BPD each year; consequently, any self-harm or suicidal thoughts in someone with BPD should be treated quickly and severely. Get assistance as soon as possible if you or someone you know is on the verge of killing themselves.

The most reasonable way for dealing with and treating BPD is psychotherapy. While there is no one-size-fits-all pharmaceutical to treat BPD, prescription medication may help with many comorbid diseases that often accompany the disorder, enhancing treatment efficacy. It's important to remember that, although these drugs can't cure BPD, they may help pave the path for more effective treatment.

While the patient is receiving normal BPD therapy, anxiety and depression are two of the most prevalent co-morbid disorders treated with medication. Antipsychotics treat psychotic, paranoid, impulsive, and melancholy symptoms and anxiety, suicidal thoughts, and wrath. It's vital to look for and treat co-morbid symptoms while working with a BPD patient. Before starting treatment, co-morbid symptoms must be treated, and therapy must begin. Substance addiction, which is often associated with BPD, should be eliminated as a factor in problematic behavior before effective therapy can begin. The patient's cognitive ability may be damaged if it isn't, making a professional's full examination difficult.

Bpd Impulsive

Impulsive borderlines are often pleasant, vibrant, and entertaining. If you're looking for thrills, you may be shallow, flirtatious, and elusive, but you'll become bored quickly. People who are borderline impulsive rely on their attention and enthusiasm to function. Therefore, they often get into trouble when they act first and consider afterward. They may seek acceptance from others to escape rejection and abandonment, leading to drug misuse and self-injurious behavior.

One of the four kinds of bipolar illness is irrational bipolar disorder. It is the busiest of the four BPD subgroups. According to psychologist Theodore Million, the impulsive subtype has a lot in common with a borderline personality disorder.

Signs and Symptoms of Impulsive BPD

The following signs and symptoms of impulsive borderline personality disorder are typical in people with this subtype:

- Pursuing pleasures and taking risks with little regard for the consequences

- Excess capacity and a propensity towards boredom

- Efforts to get people's attention

- Vanity allows individuals to be entertained on a superficial level while neglecting deeper experiences or connections.

- Animated and charismatic

- Thrilling, intriguing, and unpredictable

- When it comes to positioning oneself as the center of attention, you are dishonest to others.

- Captivating, possessing a natural affinity for chronic or recurring medical issues

- Being flirtatious with someone, even if they aren't aware of it

- The indications and symptoms of the impulsive subtype overlap or complement those of the more prevalent BPD symptoms.

Signs and Symptoms of BPD in General

Keep a watch out for the following warning signs and indicators:

- Emotional reactions that are abnormally strong concerning the source of the emotion

- Emotions that are easy to evoke

- Fear, jitters, tension, worry, and anxiety are increasing.

- Emotional state

- A tendency to exaggerate or minimize the worth of others.

- Uncertainty and fear of the unknown

- When it comes to black and white,

- Anxiety about losing control

- Excessive sensitivity to perceived rejection or criticism

- Guilty feelings that are strong and widespread

- Uncertainty about one's passions, goals, job path, or basic beliefs

- Fear of being separated

- a feeling of helplessness and despair

- State of psychosis, especially when distressed

- I'm in a bad mood

- Suicidal thoughts are a kind of suicidal behavior.

- Continual thoughts of nothingness

- Excessive self-criticism

- Having trouble coming up with or sticking to strategies

- Taking chances with things like marital promiscuity and gambling

- An unstable or poor sense of self-worth and image

- Intolerance

2.4 The Impulsive Subtype of Bpd and Its Causes

It's tough to determine the specific root of an issue in the field of mental disease. Psychiatric diseases are complicated, and much of the research needed to understand their causes better is still ongoing.

Various causes currently cause mental diseases, none of which seem to have a greater influence than others. Potential triggers are childhood injuries, neurobiological issues, neurological disorders, biology, environmental influences, socioeconomic concerns, and psychological characteristics.

BPD, the impulsive subtype, and the triggers and relationships are the subjects of many studies. You recognize the importance of the following variables:

Childhood Adversity

Childhood abuse is a common incidence among BPD patients. According to victims, violence and neglect are two of the most prevalent childhood traumas, with sexual assault most common.

In people's childhoods with BPD, researchers discovered a significant rate of caregiver failure and incest. Adults with BPD often report that their caregivers rejected their sentiments as children and failed to provide them with the protection they need. Caregivers who are emotionally distant and untrustworthy are the most typical trait among people with BPD or the impulsive subtype.

Factors in Neurobiology

BPD has been linked to abnormal estrogen levels. These hormone levels may be measured throughout a woman's menstrual cycle. On the other hand, Extreme PMS requires a different strategy than BPD, and hormone therapy should not be started in women with endometriosis.

Abnormalities of the Brain

A variety of neurological abnormalities have been discovered in people with BPD. The hippocampus and amygdala, for example, have shrunk in size. In those with BPD, the prefrontal cortex is also less present than in people who do not have the condition. Cortisol production is regulated by the hypothalamic-pituitary-adrenal axis, which is frequently enhanced in people with BPD. Cortisol overproduction might result from stressful childhood experiences that trigger cortisol production. Patients may perceive stressful conditions due to a high level of hormone production in the body.

Genetics is a branch of biology that deals with

Genetic variation is the focus of BPD causal analysis. BPD is thought to be heritable in roughly 65 percent of cases. According to research conducted in the Netherlands, hereditary influences account for 42 percent of the diversity in BPD symptoms across patients, and BPD symptoms are connected to chromosome 9. DRD4, which has similarly been linked to disordered binding, and DAT, linked to inhibitory regulatory anomalies, are two other genes being looked at for their potential involvement in BPD development.

Other Considerations

Researchers are presently investigating other variables that may contribute to BPD development. Researchers are looking at aspects such as family stability and social stability since a strong family unit may help prevent the development of this condition. They might have a role in the onset of BPD.

Diagnosing BPD of the impulsive kind

BPD has always been difficult to recognize and diagnose. Mental health practitioners have sought to describe the treatment and care for people with BPD since Adolf Stern created the term in 1938. The assessment of BPD in a therapeutic context is complicated by many factors, which adds to the difficulties.

BPD patients have a high prevalence of comorbidity. Many persons with BPD also have severe depression, depressive difficulties, drug addiction, antisocial personality disorder, and eating disorders, to name a few. Some of these concerns, such as drug misuse, may make it difficult for others to notice BPD from the outside, and some of them, such as drug abuse, can impair a person's cognitive ability and recovery.

Managing impulsive BPD

"While the ups and downs of regular life might be difficult to bear at times, medication exists that can dramatically alter how a person processes and manages their condition."

A person with BPD should seek treatment as soon as possible. Delaying therapy may exacerbate the sickness, which, if left untreated, may become severely debilitating over time. BPD is also connected to a large number of suicides each year. As a result, anybody with BPD who engages in self-harm has suicidal thoughts or engages in self-mutilation or actions should be treated and taken seriously right away. If you or someone you know is suicidal, you should get treatment from a mental health professional as soon as possible. BPD is difficult to diagnose, treat, and recover from, yet it is not untreatable. BPD may be treated, according to studies, and those who suffer from it can aim for a perfectly stable and happy life.

Psychotherapy is a form of treatment that is used.

Psychotherapy is used in a lot of BPD studies. Cognitive behavior therapy (CBT), dialectical behavior therapy (DBT), mentalization-based therapy (MBT), transference-focused therapy (TFP), schema-focused treatment (SFT), and general psychological management are some of the treatments for BPD. MBT and DBT are two of the most effective, but the key to a successful recovery is figuring out what works best for each individual.

Prescription drugs

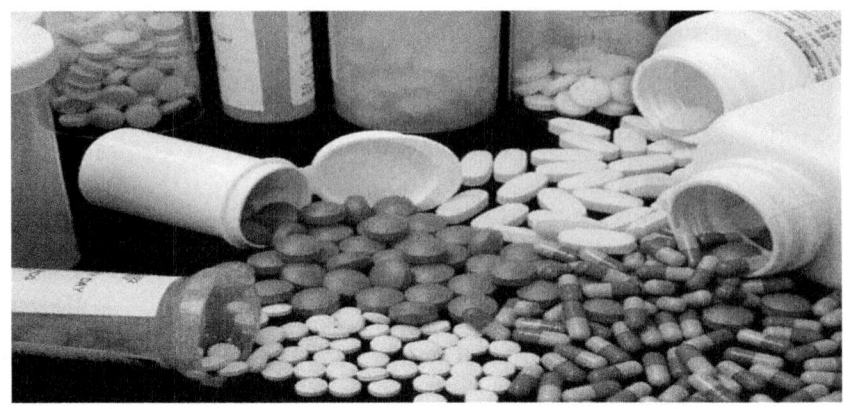

While there is no cure for BPD, medications are often used in combination with it to moderate symptoms and improve overall treatment. Anxiety, tension, rage, and impulsivity, for example, should be managed with medication when the core symptoms of BPD are addressed without the distracting effects of the other concerns. Medical management of these comorbid disorders is not only beneficial; it is also deemed necessary in the treatment of BPD. It's important to remember that, although there's no known cure for BPD, medicines may help manage the symptoms. It's only a question of establishing the framework for more efficient and effective management of the overlapping concerns.

It doesn't have to be a constant battle to live with impulsive BPD. While the ups and downs of daily life might be taxing, therapy can profoundly alter how individuals think about and deal with their issues.

The Maximum Performance Center is a pioneer in treating BPD in adolescents and young adults. Psychology Today rated the

OPI Intensive "Best of Diagnosis for BPD treatment." OPI Intensive meets the unique needs of rehabilitation group members while also offering a safe social environment for BPD patients. The curriculum consists of a 30-day immersion stage and a 30-day revolutionary phase. As a result, young people with BPD are far more equipped to manage their symptoms and operate freely and cheerfully as adults.

What is a petulant borderline personality disorder, and how does that affect you?

The cross border is characterized by unpredictability, wrath, aggression, and annoyance. Most of the time, you're obstinate, pessimistic, and bitter. You go back and forth between emotions of inadequacy and wrath. They may erupt as a result of their rage outbursts. Petulant borderlines are scared of being let down by others, yet they can't seem to shake their need to depend on people. They are passive-aggressive and may self-harm to draw attention to themselves.

How does it appear?

At 20, they sought therapy at Optimum Performance Institute for their petulant borderline personality disorder, making stable relationships almost impossible for years.

Nobody can dispute that they were brought up in a strict atmosphere. Since she was an alcoholic, their mother had never seen her father. They were taken from their home when she was six years old and their sister.

They were placed in three foster homes when their mother's parental rights were revoked. Their new "parents" were kind, assisting them with academics and incorporating her in all family events. They became used to them, but she never had a strong bond. It was a high priority for them to keep this knowledge hidden from their family. It didn't matter whether the secret was huge or little; it didn't matter. They enjoyed that they didn't have to depend on them and had no idea who she was.

"Borderline personality features should be addressed for both categories."

We liked their father, but they were uninterested in us. Her classmates were much the same, particularly as she became older. What could have been a little setback for others, such as a buddy becoming ill and having to cancel plans, turned into a nightmare for Kylie, who turned to self-harm to soothe her grief and "tell" people that she wasn't okay? They imagined their new friends to be lovely, and they warned them that if they didn't live up to her high expectations, they would be disappointed or angry, telling them that "if you cared about me, you would..." Their partners couldn't take it, and just a handful of their relationships lasted more than a year.

What are the signs and effects of petulant BPD?

Among the petulant borderline personality disorder characteristics they displayed were:

- Co-occurring disorders include things like alcohol abuse and food problems.

- Are you unhappy with your marriages?

- Suspicion of others/paranoia in relationships

- A desire to exert control over others

- Suicidal ideation

- Extreme mood swings

- The fear of being left alone.

- Issuing ultimatums in marriages as a way of "proving" that someone doesn't care for her.

- In social contexts, jittery

- Constantly seeking confirmation

- Unworthiness and unlovability feelings

- There is a lot of push and pull in relationships.

- Angry outbursts

- wishing for individuals to be repentant for their actions (or lack thereof)

- a reluctance to share one's ideas

- Isolating oneself from the rest of the world.

- Suicidal or self-injurious behaviors were used to gain influence over others.

Fear of abandonment, low self-esteem, and difficulty self-soothe drive certain BPD behaviors. With the appropriate therapy, you can overcome petulant BPD.

What is the only way to deal with a defiant BPD diagnosis?

They attended two outpatient BPD clinics as kids. Despite this, they received scant help. They taught about mental diseases and recognizing signs, but not how their issues would affect their long-term ambitions. They lacked the motivation to engage in BPD treatment.

After a 20-year-old student committed suicide in their campus residence, they were ordered to leave college. Our focus on assisting young people with BPD in their rehabilitation and transition to adulthood seemed more appropriate, so they picked the Optimum Performance Institute.

After she started at OPI, they worked closely with their psychiatrist to better grasp their BPD symptoms and issues.

They used dialectical behavior therapy (DBT) procedures until they became automatic. They used self-soothing strategies to learn to regulate their emotions.

Their doctor and they decided they could go deep into the occurrences. Their therapist didn't think they were ready to manage until they had enough real-life experience with dialectical behavior modification strategies.

It was challenging to open those wounds and examine the emotions and thoughts they held. Coworkers at OPI who had been through similar experiences urged her to get over it. Every week, they traveled to the beach and took part in a hip-hop class to relax.

They didn't have to wait long to put their new capabilities, especially their interpersonal skills, to the test. They got a job at a pet shop because they wanted to be vets. They met with the director of education until the new school year to prepare their veterinary school curriculum. They took a few courses at a nearby community college and spoke to their OPI life coach about the best research techniques.

They studied and worked for eight months while balancing school, jobs, relationships, and treatment. They were ready to go home, knowing what prompted their BPD symptoms and how to deal with them. They wanted to build on her career, college, and OPI ties when they returned home.

"Petulant BPD is seldom treated alone."

What is the only way to get treatment with petulant BPD?

BPD is notoriously tough to manage alone. Borderline personality disorder symptoms may cause great pain, often leading to the same monster you're trying to avoid: unhealthy relationships.

Call us right now at 855.697.6498 for assistance with BPD symptoms, co-occurring diseases, and improving relationships. We'd want to learn more about your treatment needs and see whether ours is a good match.

Chapter 3: BPD & Suicide

Suicide is more common in those with a borderline personality disorder. These people must be distinguished from those who have conventional mood disorders and are suicidal simply because they are sad.

A borderline personality disorder is characterized by suicidality (BPD). It's also the aspect that causes the most concern in those who work with this condition. Patients with BPD who have never experienced a depressive episode are uncommon. According to DSM-IV-TR criteria, these people experience "recurrent suicide actions, movements, or attacks, or self-mutilating behavior, " Patients often have suicidal thoughts and threats, and the majority of them attempt suicide many times. Suicide attempts are prevalent in BPD patients and may last for years (months - years). Patients with "BPD" are distinguished from "normal mood disorders," who are only suicidal due to excessive stress. Though "BPD" sometimes starts in childhood with recurring suicide attempts and lasts until "early adulthood," these inclinations usually fade with time. Suicidal ideas come and go throughout time, rising when "life" is complex and fading when it isn't.

Suicide is linked to emotional instability in "BPD" sufferers. "BPD" produces rapid mood shifts in response to life events, rather than long-term depression or mania that lasts weeks or months. The lack of mood in "BPD" to respond consistently to "antidepressants" demonstrates the distinct symptoms. Suicidal behavior has been linked to impulsive personality traits. According to Soloff and colleagues, patients with BPD had a (mean) number of lifetime attempts, and the number of attempts was connected to impulsive levels.

3.1 Suicide completion in "BPD."

Long-term naturalistic follow-up studies suggest that 10% of people with BPD commit suicide, whereas 90% do not. Suppression of the stigma of mental illness may help reduce the stigma of mental illness.

The age at which "suicide" conclusions emerge in "BPD" investigations is one of the most intriguing results. Threats and attempts peak early in BPD development (borderline personality disorder), although finalization occurs later. De facto, many with BPD "kill" themselves later in the illness, generally when they cannot recover. In one study, patients who died by suicide were 30, whereas they were 37 (SD, 10) years old in another. Clinicians should also keep in mind that it's impossible to predict precise conditions due to the rarity of completions.

3.2 The meaning of suicidality in "BPD."

Secret drug addiction is the most common suicidal behavior in BPD. These overdoses frequently involve a warning to a lover or psychiatrist. BPD patients are more likely to slit their wrists and engage in other self-destructive behaviors. However, self-mutilation is not considered a form of suicide. It involves minor incisions on the wrists and sides, and patients say it helps relieve acute dysphoric symptoms. 9,27% "Self-mutilation" may lead to addiction.

"BPD" patients employ suicidal thoughts and actions for different causes.

The first is to empower you. If you can't manage your own life, you may at least threaten to die. The second is to have a soothing path out of anguish and suffering. Step three is to express your displeasure. Patients with "BPD" don't want to be easily understood; therefore, they measure their pain.

3.3 The management of "chronic" suicidality

Therapists dislike borderline patients because suicidality scares them. Its probable "therapists" fear being sued if a suicide occurs. On the other hand, Suicidality is a distinct concern in BPD patients and should be handled.

Most vital. The coping skills for acute suicidality should not be employed for persistent suicidality. Most BPD specialists encourage clinicians to accept suicidality and address the underlying issues. Active suicide prevention approaches fail in "BPD" patients because they prolong the symptoms they are designed to cure.)

Kornberg says clinicians should tell patients and families they can't be held accountable for or prevent suicide. In contrast, Malts Berger says clinicians must accept a calculated risk to treat BPD patients properly.

Many people feel that hospitalization should be avoided. Linehan believes hospitalization hinders recovery and plans to stay just one night. Hospitalization should be utilized as a last resort, says Livesey. Dawson and MacMillan said "BPD" sufferers should never be hospitalized.

While Gunderson does not rule out entrance, he informs them that it would be fruitless. The APA's clinical guidelines for BPD constitute a jury agreement and a distinct opinion. If the patient's health is in jeopardy, hospitalization may be advised.

Unproven techniques have not been shown to improve safety or reduce mortality.

Also, chronic suicide is more likely to need "hospitalization." Even after being hospitalized, most patients still have suicidal thoughts. Frequent hospitalizations might disrupt a patient's routine. There is a practical and evidence-based alternative. Outpatient therapy for BPD in Distress is effective in trials. There are several benefits to day clinics over a (full) hospital stay.

Most "BPD" patients get "psychotherapy" as "outpatients" to curb impulsivity. But there's no proof that drugs can stop suicide. Rather than preventing suicide, successful BPD therapy may address the underlying issues that contribute to suicidal thoughts. DBT (dialectical behavior treatment) reduces suicidal thoughts.

Using DBT, clinicians undertake clinical research to verify suicidal anxiety, identify the causes that cause Distress, and explore possible treatments. Instead, then "reinforcing" suicidality with additional therapist contact, DBT delivers negative feedback (temporary loss of sessions) for suicidal behaviors (a common problem with most treatments).

More recently, therapeutic studies have been conducted on mentalization-based counseling, transference-dependent therapy, and schema therapy. Surveillance data shows that most recovered BPD patients are working, half are in happy relationships, and one-quarter have children. However, no comprehensive study has established if their children are still at risk.

3.4 Three Major Risk Factors for Suicide in BPD (borderline personality disorder)

Three symptoms may help clinicians detect suicidal patients getting DBT (dialectical behavior therapy). Large longitudinal research found that people with BPD attempted suicide more than those with avoidant, schizotypal, or OCPD (obsessive-compulsive-personality-disorder).

The research discovered three key (independent) risk factors for suicide attempts within the DSM-5 diagnostic criteria for borderline personality disorder. Afraid of abandonment, identity issues, "chronic feelings" of desolation, etc. "The take-home message for clinicians is to test for these three characteristics in BPD patients when assessing suicide risk," says study researcher Shirley Yen, Ph.D.

Unique Features

Mentally sick people are more likely to commit suicide. Patients with BPD, on the other hand, are at greater risk, regardless of their "psychiatric comorbidities."

The researchers examined data from the "Collaborative Longitudinal Study of Personality Disorders," which included persons with one of the four personality disorders and a group of "match controls" with some severe depressive condition (MDD).

Earlier results from this research linked emotional instability and depression to suicide attempts at 2 and 7 years. "Most attention on BPD and suicide risk has been on effective dysfunction and impulsivity. So they set out to discover all of "BPD's" distinctive characteristics, "Yen noted.

Seven hundred one people came from inpatient, partial, and outpatient care establishments. The group was 33 years old, 64% female, 70% white, 73% educated, and 62% unemployed. The reference group had MDD but little PD (less than 2 criteria). "The MDD population was compared to all other PD populations, but not to BPD. Since all categories may meet any criteria, the study combines them all. For additional (variable) parameter distributions, "Yen noted.

Fold Increased Risk

We used the Diagnostic Consultation for DIPD (DSM-IV-Personality-Disorders) and the Schedule for Non-adaptive &

Adaptive Personality to assess participants at baseline. Suicidality was examined at every stage.

Suicidal intent was discovered in 21% of study participants throughout ten years. Suicide attempts were shown to be connected to the female sex, poorer education, and unemployment, with each component resulting in a 1.5-fold increased risk. Despite being the most common ailment among PD and MDD patients, MDD is not a substantial risk factor for suicide attempts in the general population.

Under normal circumstances, a history of childhood sexual abuse or neglect was a substantial risk factor for suicide attempts, increasing the chances of attempting suicide by nearly 2.5 times. A 6.5-fold increase in the likelihood of suicidal failure was seen in BPD, even after excluding the self-injury condition. OCPD had the lowest risk.

Risk of the Suicide Attempts affected by Personality Disorder:

Personality Disorder	Odds Ratio (95% CI)
BPD	6.53 (4.33 - 9.85)
BPD (without self-injury)	4.99 (3.35 - 7.41)
OCPD	0.47 (0.31 - 0.71)

Researchers next used two distinct trials to see whether BPD features were linked to suicide attempts, with both models adjusting for demographic and mental factors. The first model evaluated each BPD criterion separately, while the second model estimated all BPD traits simultaneously (excluding self-injurious behavior). When each condition was taken into account independently, the likelihood of suicide rose by two or three times.

Only three parameters emerged as major independent causes (correlated) with suicidal attempts over time in the simultaneous model: identity disorder (OR, 2.21; 95 percent CI, 1.37 - 3.56), frantic attempts to avoid abandonment (OR, 1.93; 95 percent CI, 1.17 - 3.16), and persistent (feelings) of emptiness (OR, 1.93; 95 percent CI, 1.17 - 3.16). (OR, 1.93; 95 percent CI, 1.17 - 3.16). (OR: 1.93; 95 percent confidence interval: 1.17 - 3.16). (Odds ratio: 1.63; 95% confidence interval: 1.03 to 2.57)

"We may put forth some possibilities," Yen said, adding that further research is needed to figure out why personality disturbance, persistent (feelings) of emptiness and desperate attempts to escape alienation led to suicidality.

These three parameters, which correspond to personality processing disruptions in the DSM-5 Another Model of "Personality Disorders," are "likely to have a major persistent effect on an individual's "interpersonal functioning," which can manifest itself in a variety of ways, including social exclusion, loneliness, and a sense of belonging," she said.

Painful Symptoms

According to Donald W. Black, MD, professor emeritus, Iowa City, in a statement to "Medscape" Medical News, the study "confirms that BPD is a substantial component in suicide attempts and contributes to our knowledge of the symptoms associated with it." According to Black, who was not engaged in the research, these symptoms are "painful." They "may underpin the person's interpersonal issues," according to Black, and "may collide with self-direction and interest in aims." Since specialized therapies for BPD are available, clinicians should inquire about BPD symptoms among sad patients or have attempted suicide. Furthermore, according to the research, "the physician may desire to inquire directly about these three symptoms and explain their relevance to the patient."

Grants from the National Institute of Mental Health, Columbia University, the (New York State) NYS Psychiatric Institute, HMS/McLean Hospital, Yale University, Vanderbilt University, and Brown University supported the research. During his research, yen received help from Janssen and funding from the "National Institute of Mental Health."

Demographic and mental characteristics such as childhood sexual assault, alcohol and opiate use disorders, and posttraumatic stress disorder were included as covariates (PTSD).

3.5 Elements of BPD may increase the risk for suicide attempts.

According to research published in JAMA Psychiatry, specific aspects of BPD may enhance the likelihood of suicide attempts.

"They had a rare opportunity to explore which features of BPD projected suicidal behavior over the ten years of follow-up," "Shirley Yen," (Ph.D., of the 'Massachusetts Mental Health Center' at Harvard Medical School), told, "Healio Psychiatry," "Because their research involved collecting ten years of evidence, they had a rare opportunity to explore which features of BPD projected suicidal behavior over the ten years "

Because their study required 10 years of data collection, they had a unique chance to investigate whether characteristics were present." if they wanted to see whether there were any characteristics that were associated to suicide attempts among participants in the "Collaborative Longitudinal Study" of Personality Disorders, with a focus on BPD and its criteria, over ten years.

Adults with four distinct personality disorders and a control group with MDD and lower personality disorder traits were studied in the CLPS. A total of 701 people responded to at least one of the follow-up surveys. Researchers performed (year) semi-structured diagnostic interviews and used a range of self-report evaluations, as well as multiple logistic regression models, to identify baseline demographic and clinical risk factors of suicide attempts across a ten-year prospective follow-up period.

BPD was shown to be the most significant predictor of prospectively reported suicide attempts (OR = 4.18; 95 percent CI, 2.68-6.52) despite adjusting for other relevant characteristics such as sex, employment, education, childhood sexual abuse, and PTSD.

When other important causes and BPD criteria were controlled for, identity disturbance (OR = 2.21; 95 percent CI, 1.37-3.56), chronic feelings of emptiness (OR = 1.63; 95 percent CI, 1.03-2.57), and frantic efforts to avoid rejection (OR = 1.93; 95 percent CI, 1.17-3.16) were the significant independent factors related to suicidal attempts over time.

"Identity disruption, persistent feelings of emptiness, and desperate attempts to prevent abandonment are all understudied and perhaps underestimated 'risk factors for suicide ideation," Yen added. "This may also help explain why BPD is so closely linked to suicide conduct," the researcher says. In addition to effective dysfunction and impulsivity (both of which are suicide risk factors in other disorders), the other three criteria in the Alternative Model of Personality Disorders in DSM-5 Section 3 that reflect personality functioning abnormalities are fairly unique to BPD and warrant further consideration in suicide risk assessments."

Chapter 4: Diagnosis, Treatment, and Management of BPD

4.1 Diagnosis of BPD

One of the most disputed types of personality disorder is borderline personality disorder (BPD). The clinical diagnosis's validity and reliability and the construct's value have been questioned. Furthermore, it is questionable how well research or clinical diagnoses reflect the experiences of those diagnosed with personality disorders.

According to a substantial body of research, BPD overlaps significantly with other personality disorders categories, with 'pure' borderline personality disorder (BPD) present in just three to ten percent of cases. There are several variations in clinical studies (narcissistic, histrionic, and antisocial). Furthermore, borderline personality disorder (BPD), anxiety, and mood disorders have many commonalities.

The DSM-IV diagnostic criteria for BPD are included in this guideline (APA, 1994). (See Table 1) The core characteristics of BPD, according to the DSM-IV, include instability in interpersonal relationships, self-image and mood, and marked impulsivity starting in early adulthood.

Table 1 DSM-IV standards for BPD (APA, 1994)

	A persistent configuration of interpersonal relationship ambiguity, self-image & emotions, and seeming impulsivity that starts in early adulthood and emerges in a range of circumstances is described by five (or more) of the following:
1.	feverish endeavors to prevent perceived or actual defection Note: Self-mutilation and suicidal behavior are not included in criterion 5.
2.	A depiction of strong and uncomfortable interpersonal connections typified by an uneasy balance of devaluation and idealization.
3.	A constantly and significantly shifting sense of self or self-image is a symptom of identity difficulties.

4.	Impulsivity in two or more sections can be self-destructive (spending, substance abuse, sex, binge eating, and reckless driving). Note: Self-mutilation and suicidal behavior are not included in criterion 5.
5.	Suicidal behavior, threats, gestures, or self-mutilation occur regularly.
6.	A high emotional reactivity causes affective ambiguity (for instance, extreme episodic dysphoria, anxiety, and irritability frequently lasting for a few hours & only infrequently more than rare days).
7.	Feelings of emptiness occur regularly.
8.	Inappropriate conduct includes anger control disorders, rage outbursts, and excessive fury (for instance, recurrent presentations of temper, recurring physical fights, constant anger).
9.	Suspicious creativity, as well as transient or severe dissociative episodes, are all provoked by stress.

Although the International Classification of Diseases, 10th revision (ICD-10; WHO, 1992) does not have a separate category for BPD, it does have a related disorder called "emotionally dysfunctional personality disorder and borderline type" (F 60.31), which is characterized by inconsistency in attitudes, relationships, and self-image. Transitory quasi-psychotic symptoms are not included in ICD-10 (criterion nine of DSM-IV group). When comparing ICD and DSM criteria for a similar set of patients, it was discovered that there was no overlap between the two systems. In a sample of fifty-two outpatients examined using both methodologies, only roughly one-third of the competitors was diagnosed with the same major personality disorder. More changes to the DSM and ICD are needed to simplify integrating the two categories, albeit this is unlikely to change the current personality disorder definition.

The use of organized interview schedules has greatly increased the accuracy of personality disorder diagnosis. Excessive interview time is a common issue with many of them, even though no one plan has been designated as the "gold standard," since each has its own set of benefits and drawbacks. (Table 2 shows the most often used tools for measuring BPD.) Both schedules accurately diagnose BPD when used by a highly trained rater. Despite this, only a limited degree of consensus exists over the whole interview program.

Additionally, the clinical and testing approaches used to identify personality disorders differ. Even though most contemporary instruments rely on simple questions from the DSM-IV, clinicians have discovered that straight questions are only marginally efficient in identifying personality disorders.

Instead, clinicians are more likely to identify patients with a personality disorder after listening to them speak about their interpersonal interactions and seeing their behavior.

Table 2 The chief instruments presented for assessment of BPD

Diagnostic Discussion for **DSM-IV** Personality Disorders (DIPD-IV)
Structured Clinical Interview for **DSM-IV** Personality Disorders (SCID-II)
Structured Interview for **DSM-IV** Personality **(SIDP-IV)**
International Personality Disorder Examination **(IPDE)**
Personality Assessment Schedule **(PAS)**
Standardized Assessment of Personality (SAP)

BPD diagnosis is typically based on a formless clinical examination outside of specialized treatment settings. This strategy, however, has several limitations. There is evidence that doctors' diagnoses of personality disorders are inconsistent, for starters. Second, the existence of a major physical or mental illness might influence personality evaluation. An initial diagnosis of BPD may only be made in the absence of mental or physical disorders. Psychosis, substance addiction, affective and anxiety problems, and surgical or medical condition experience are possible signs of BPD. Before obtaining a conclusive diagnosis of BPD, clinicians may get an informant description of their personality.

All personality disorders are consistent throughout time. Personality disorders are classified as having continuous traits in the DSM and ICD classifications. Few longitudinal studies on personality disorders have supported the idea of BPD as a persistent entity until recently. Over the last ten years, studies on the issue have shown a wide range of stability estimations. According to recent projected changes, many people diagnosed with BPD would not consistently stay at the diagnostic threshold, even for a short period. Even though individual variances in personality disorder traits are rather stable, the overall number of criteria used seems to fluctuate significantly over time. Reclassification is essential because of the many issues with BPD diagnosis, which will probably occur with the publishing of DSM-V.

4.2 Bpd Management and Treatment

1. Current outline of services

In adult population mental health care in the United Kingdom and Wales, people with personality disorders get varying therapy degrees. In the United Kingdom and Wales, personality disorder efforts are a major part of the healthcare system. Because the decision to increase efforts to provide personality disorder therapy was first taken in 2003, the implementation of these services has been uneven and, in some circumstances, unsatisfactory. While these programs are intended to help people with personality disorders, most people who seek them out have BPD, which the healthcare system recognizes. In the United Kingdom, the project aids in the development of innovative psychosocial recovery therapies, public health pilot programs, and an education and training approach. The major goal is to expand the capacity for one-of-a-kind personality services throughout the country.

2. Pharmacological therapy

Co-morbid mental disorders such as bipolar disorder, depression, PTSD, drug addiction, and psychosis are more common among people with BPD than in the general population; the lifetime prevalence of at least one co-morbid psychological disease in this group approaches 100%. Furthermore, several state-and-trait-associated BPD symptoms (such as affective impairment, intermittent stress-linked psychotic symptoms, self-harming and suicidal behaviors, and irritability) are similar to those of other mental illnesses and may, on the surface, respond appropriately to drug therapy.

Antidepressants, antipsychotics, and mood stabilizers are often used in therapeutic settings. According to a comprehensive examination of US prescription systems, 10% of persons with BPD were prescribed an antipsychotic, 27% were prescribed a mood stabilizer, 35% were prescribed an antianxiety medication, and 61% have prescribed an antidepressant at some point during their treatment. The average number of antidepressant prescriptions for bipolar disorder seemed twice as high. Although there are few published studies of clinical practices in the United Kingdom, there is no reason to believe that if patients with this disease seek treatment, psychotropic drug prescription in the UK varies from that in the United States. The placebo effect is frequent in this scenario; the crisis is generally short and may be anticipated to resolve without the need for drugs.

To minimize more transient, stress-related adverse effects, the prescription medication is frequently maintained, and if they arise, another drug from a different group may be prescribed. Longitudinal research found that 75% of people with BPD were given drug combinations at some time throughout their therapy. Individuals who have many crises visits to the hospital may get repeated mental medications in conjunction with other therapies for minor physical problems. Medication adherence is often poor over time, and frequent changes in prescriptions make it difficult to determine which treatments, if any, have benefited and in what ways.

Many psychiatric medications now on the market have clinically significant side effects. Antipsychotic medications, for example, may cause significant weight gain, aggravate self-esteem issues, and increase the risk of major medical illnesses such as cardiovascular disease and diabetes. Lithium may be the cause of hypothyroidism. When used in excess, valproate may cause weight gain and is a known human teratogen. Still, selective serotonin reuptake inhibitors can cause unpleasant withdrawal symptoms if not taken regularly. The risks of selective inhibitors of serotonin reuptake, which have been linked to therapy-developing suicidal thoughts in young adults, may outweigh the benefits, and valproate can sometimes increase the risk of polycystic ovaries in young females, so the benefits and drawbacks of psychotropic drugs are usually worse in teenagers and young adults.

While many psychotropic drugs have wide product licenses that cover certain indications or symptom clusters, no psychotropic treatment has been expressly approved to treat BPD. Mood stabilizers, antidepressants, and antipsychotics will be given according to their authorized indications if co-morbid depression, paranoia, or bipolar illness is detected. Psychotropic drugs are mostly "off-label" or unlicensed when psychotic or depressive symptoms or impairment in functioning do not meet diagnostic criteria for mental disease. Off-label prescribing increases the prescriber's obligations and may enhance the prescriber's accountability if side effects occur. At the very least, off-label advice should follow a well-established body of medical knowledge and be rational. The Royal College of Psychiatrists advises informing patients that the medicine they are receiving is not FDA-approved and thoroughly explaining the purpose for use and any possible side effects.

1. Psychological interventions

Treatment strategies for persons with BPD have a long history of influencing people's perceptions of the disorder. BPD was included in DSM-III in 1980, but not in ICD-10, because of the emerging psychoanalytic idea of 'borderline personality association,' which is halfway between insanity and neurosis. As a result, the notion of BPD was first popularized in the United States, and it was not widely recognized in the United Kingdom until the mid-1980s. Many experiential, psychodynamic, behavioral, and cognitive-behavioral therapies were offered within NHS mental health hospitals at the time, but they were few. Cognitive therapy for depression was also in its infancy at the time. Many persons with BPD suffer from behavioral, depressive, and anxiety disorders, and they've been treated using these treatments. Therapists adopted these strategies to help persons with more complicated psychological disorders in the 1980s and 1990s, and systematic processes were created expressly for this client group.

As a result, unique treatments for BPD have been established by changing conventional techniques. Psychoanalytic techniques were changed in the United States and the United Kingdom to include more confinement, structure (formal contracts between therapist and client), and responsiveness. The classic policy of therapist neutrality and abstinence, for example, has been updated to include more psychoanalysts. A therapeutic technique based on progressive attachment theory was developed (but not identical) to traditional analytic methodology and aimed at a precise mentalization-focused treatment. Dialectical behavior therapy arose from a behavioral approach to self-harm and suicidality that included emotional control skills teaching and client practice confirmation. Through theoretical and practical exposure to partly detached mental states and their functional assessment, cognitive analytic therapy, which had first targeted interpersonal difficulties, gained more amazing applications to borderline illnesses. CT was first developed to treat depression, but it was soon expanded to include the treatment of personality disorders. One strategy, for example, focused on the early maladaptive images that underpin cognitive biases. CBT and interpersonal therapy have been altered since then (IPT). Some of these reduced therapies are provided in psychiatric rehabilitation programs (e.g., mentalization-based limited hospitalization and DBT). In contrast, others are available as one-on-one or community treatments with a more direct time limit (CAT or CBT).

Despite developments in these precise psychological therapies, most NHS-provided "talking sessions" for persons with BPD are standardized or eclectic, with no defined pattern. Clinical psychologists are educated to address a variety of evaluation, treatment, and rehabilitation requirements via therapy formulation, recovery planning, people management, and environmental change. Before they may list as practitioners, chartered clinical and counseling psychologists must complete training in two evidence-based psychological therapies, as well as further post-criterion training, according to the British Psychological Association. They don't use a certain strategy during therapy sessions, and if they do, it may not be in the best format, as shown by medical research. DBT is a therapeutic counseling program involving one-on-one treatment sessions, psychoeducational clusters, and telephone assistance from a team of therapists. Even though NHS therapists have been educated in the approach, ensuring that all aspects of DBT are accessible in practice has proven to be a practical difficulty.

In the NHS, clinical psychologists and other psychological therapy experts such as social workers, physicians, nurses, and other mental health psychotherapists provide psychological and psychosocial therapies in various venues. Individual and group therapies may be used in psychiatry and psychotherapy departments, day programs, and community mental health institutes. There have been several day programs built with particular programming experience for this client group, with some of them concentrating on therapeutic community ideas, but they are not widely accessible. A limiting element in ensuring that these treatments are accessible in practice is the relatively limited number of NHS practitioners who are properly educated to provide psychological therapy. Another difficulty is incorporating psychiatric treatment into general health and social care programs, which demands collaboration among staff from several organizations who are psychologically oblivious of the illness's existence. A psychological remedies paradigm might be applied in the treatment program using interdisciplinary squad-based training. Traditional notions of BPD as irreversible have been called into question by the development of at least partially effective psychiatric therapies, as well as a better understanding of the progressive causes and psychological processes that underpin this condition, as well as an epidemiological study on its natural history. Previous decades' clinical nihilism has given way to a conviction that psychological therapies will play a key role in the overall diagnosis, treatment, and rehabilitation of persons suffering from these disorders.

2. Arts therapies

The majority of art treatments were created in the United States and Europe. They've also been seen in treatment programs for people with personality disorders like BPD. Art therapy, theatre therapy, dance movement therapy, and music therapy are four art therapies that use art media as their primary means of communication. All four are now available in the UK. Once a week, art lessons last around an hour and a half to two hours. Patients are evaluated to see whether joining a community (typically a group of four to six persons) or undergoing independent therapy will be beneficial. The main goal is to encourage growth and development via art in a secure and friendly setting with the help of a therapist. Art therapy may benefit those who find it difficult to express their ideas and feelings verbally. Art therapy often deals with "pre-verbal" expressive material in the environment that may be explored and rationalized. The meaning of the therapist's work may be similar to psychoanalytic interpretations, or it may be less interpretive and more positive for patients to absorb what they wish to learn from the work. It is well acknowledged that "plunging explanations" without sufficient assistance is unlikely to be useful for persons with more severe BPD.

The process of producing something and the emotional responses and social dynamics that accompany it are increasingly important in arts interventions. It might be figurative, metaphorical, comical, symbolic, or contribute directly to feelings that need to be understood. More discussion and, if necessary, the use of art materials may aid in this comprehension.

3. Therapeutic communities

A therapeutic communal is a social environment that has been purposefully built and structured inside a housing or day unit to harness the social and group mechanisms for therapeutic purposes. In the healing environment, the civic is the primary therapeutic tool. In the form we know today, therapeutic groups first appeared in England during World War II at Northfield Military Hospital in Mill Hill, Birmingham, London. Psychotherapists from the Tavis tock Clinic and Cassel Hospital performed the Northfield investigations, which tremendously impacted psychoanalysis and group therapy in the United Kingdom. The Mill Hill program for battle-scarred troops resulted in the establishment of Henderson Hospital and the construction of a global "social psychiatry" metric, leading to substantially more psychiatric and less correctional care of psychological hospital patients throughout the Western world.

Consequently, various therapeutic organizations have sprung up to assist persons with personality disorders. Personality problem therapeutic communities vary from full-time rehabilitation clinics to units that run for a few hours once a week. Because the community is the main therapeutic negotiator, most programs include a variety of group therapies. Small analytic groups, psychodrama, transactional analysis, median analytic groups, arts interventions, CT, relational issue resolution, psychoeducation, and gestalt are just a few of the options. There are group meetings and activities in addition to individual treatment.

Rather than simple inclusion and rejection criteria, therapeutic communities normally use a complicated admission method. It causes diagnostic uncertainty, and there is no one-size-fits-all treatment for BPD. According to recent research, admission features suggest multiple levels of personality illness, with the majority displaying sufficient indicators to diagnose more than three personality disorders, typically in several clusters. Before the ultimate treatment program starts, the admission involves commitment, evaluation, planning, and placement stages. It's a tiered treatment strategy in which service users choose when and where they want to go to the next stage of the program. Current organization members often vote in a specially scheduled case meeting or admissions panel to accept new members. Programs and their different phases have time limits, and none of the personality disorder management groups are open-ended. Some organizations provide service users or staff-led structured or unstructured post-therapy sessions. Most of the therapeutic community's staff members are from the mental health care field, including direct medical input and professional psychotherapists. As part of socio-therapy, which is less visible than single therapies, staff will fulfill various responsibilities. As "social therapists," they often hire unskilled people with the right personality traits and ex-service members. Specific systems are often utilized to support the diverse employee functions, such as job descriptions that describe their varied tasks, equally agreed-upon protocols for dealing with various day-to-day difficulties, and strict oversight techniques.

The therapy method draws on various theoretical frameworks, including systematic, cognitive-behavioral, psychodynamic, community analytic, and humanistic traditions. In the 1950s, anthropological approaches were used to investigate the original treatment group idea at Henderson Hospital, and four key "themes" were found. Among the subjects discussed are truth-telling, democracy, permissiveness, and communalism. The more recent approach stresses the network of mutually advantageous and challenging interactions among members and the authorizing capability of followers who are held accountable for themselves and one another. It has been simplified to a basic progressive model of expressive growth.

The healing community tries to rebuild a network of intimate connections analogous to a family through which deeply established behavior patterns, negative cognitions, and negative emotions may be re-learned. Non-residential groups with personality disorders are generally found in NHS traditional mental health institutions, while housing units are common in both NHS and tier 3 organizations. In violation of these requirements, all NHS clinical communities for personality illness engage in an annual assessment cycle of peer review, self-review, and action planning to preserve uniformity and consistency of practice. The English Department of Health has authorized the development of "NHS ordering criteria," which will serve as the foundation for community therapeutic accreditation.

4.3 Other therapies

This section discusses a variety of BPD treatments that aren't covered by standard psychiatric care. Analytic, integrative & humanistic psychotherapy and systematic counseling are often used to treat personality problems. In less complicated cases, as stand-alone managements, or as part of multidisciplinary care packages or long-term therapies – in more severe or intractable illnesses.

Analytic group psychotherapy

It's often called "community counseling," broken down into non-directive categories (deprived of pre-determined programs). An important therapeutic strategy is an interaction between the participants, members, and the psychotherapist ('conductor'). In general and design, such courses promote a strong feeling of community while also being helpful and demanding. A group's membership is usually stable, with each member remaining for an average of two to five years. Suitably trained group psychotherapists (as defined by the UK Council for Psychotherapy [UKCP]) have completed at least four years of training, are subject to daily clinical regulation, and participate in ongoing professional development (CPD). Individual treatment for people with severe personality disorders may lead to potentially dangerous encounters between the therapist and the client. With the help of the group process, this may be prevented. They will effectively resolve interpersonal difficulties in the community "in real-time" and prevent confronting reliance by encouraging members to embrace personal responsibility by first sharing accountability for one another and then learning to ask for aid adaptively. Fear of personal exposure makes it difficult to begin contributing; it's also difficult to find an appropriate, acceptable meeting location; and concerns about secrecy.

Humanistic & integrative psychotherapies

Treatments are based on various theoretical frameworks that emerged in the mid-twentieth century as alternatives to psychoanalysis' dominant paradigm. There is a lot of overlap in the phrase "active remedies," which is becoming more popular.

Psychodrama is a group-based therapy that aims to comprehend brutal past emotional events and link them to current complications and worries; transactional analysis is based on parent, adult, and child' ego states' and can be done independently or in clusters, and gestalt therapy aims to facilitate the understanding of complicated past emotional episodes and link them to current complications and worries.

Systemic therapy

When the index patient is a woman, this is most often used for work with her family. It tries to help individuals overcome issues a single family member faces or the whole family by maximizing family strengths and resilience. It helps family members and caregivers better know how they work together and develop more efficient ways of communicating with and aiding one another. It follows a schedule of long yet dispersed sessions, such as two hours every six weeks. It necessitates the existence of a supervisory committee that watches or listens in on the live session, arguing ideas about how the system works and attempting to improve it. Individuals, their families, and support systems access the team's ideas and hypotheses, allowing various thoughts and viewpoints to be heard. The therapists assist the family in achieving the therapeutic objectives that they have established. Milan, social constructionist, narrative, and solution-based forms of systemic theory and interventions, as well as institutional and strategic models, are examples of these. Circular questioning (for example, "what does your brother think about your mother's response to that question?"), reframing and mapping the scheme with genograms (a pictorial depiction of a patient's family relations), and reframing and mapping the scheme with genograms (a pictorial depiction of a patient's family relations) are all examples systemic strategic or systemic approaches. When a family's dynamics are involved in maintaining or worsening the presenting variety of issues, and family members may participate, systemic treatment may aid in building new coping methods within the self-sustaining family.

Nidotherapy

Nidotherapy differs from other therapeutic techniques in that it focuses on environmental adjustments to improve a person's fit with their surroundings. Nidotherapy is derived from nidus Latin, which means "to nest." It is not a therapy in this sense. Still, it does have the therapeutic goal of improving the value of life by accepting a degree of handicap and adaptability to the environment.

Chapter 5: Recovery in BPD

5.1 Background

The term "recovery" has long been used to describe symptom improvement and the absence of medical criteria in BPD (BPD). Diagnostic remission is widespread in longitudinal investigations, ranging from 33 to 99 percent. On the other hand, personal rehabilitation regards transformation as a process rather than a finished product. The CHIME paradigm (connectedness, hope, identity, meaning, and empowerment) was formed through conceptual models of personal recovery. The mental health approach to people with BPD needs further research. The restoration of self and other perspectives is characterized as recovery in a qualitative study of personality disorders. Castillo et al. characterized rehabilitation as a hierarchical phase that establishes stable attachment patterns and ends with transformative recovery. This time created hope, goals, identities, obligations, and a sense of belonging. Mood regulation and other symptoms were aims of Kataoka and colleagues. A study of BPD patients revealed that, in addition to symptom reduction, objectives included creating connections, having a sense of self, and improving one's health. While these results suggest that manualized treatments' therapeutic aims may be limited, comprehending personality disorder rehabilitation is complicated by overlapping psychiatric and personal therapy domains. Treatment will be more personalized when personality disorders are conceptualized in a dimensional framework that emphasizes individual features, severity, and functioning. A lot of people seeking professional aid have found their perspectives properly reflected. While specialized facilities are required, a wider approach that includes people who cannot access or no longer use them may offer a fuller picture. It conforms with recommendations for better understanding opposing viewpoints on therapy. Thus, this research seeks to learn more about BPD patients' rehabilitation experiences and viewpoints at various stages of recovery. Participants in the restored and unrecovered courses were compared to validate shifts.

5.2 Methodology (Participants and inclusion)

Individuals were first approached through behavioral health groups and social media to engage in an online experiment, utilizing previously used strategies in personality disorder research. The research's inclusion criteria are based on the literature's understanding that rehabilitation occurs at different times and in different ways. After a two-year follow-up period, half of the participants in a randomized trial of adults with schizophrenia did not go beyond the first stage of rehabilitation ('overwhelmed by the impairment'). Nobody made it to the end of the healing process ('living outside the handicap'). According to research on BPD treatment, the last stage ('recovered') is even more uncertain. As a result, understanding the viewpoints of persons at various stages of BPD therapy may be crucial. After completing an online survey, researchers divided people into four groups based on their recovery and clinical status. The recovery status of individuals was assessed by comparing BPD rehabilitation criteria to their own. The McLean BPD Screening Instrument was used to identify whether or not someone had BPD (MSI-BPD). The MSI-BPD is a ten-item self-report screening test that indicates a high possibility of fulfilling DSM-5 BPD criteria with a score of 7 or above. With good sensitivity (0.81), accuracy (0.85), and persistence (alpha = 0.74), the MSI-BPD demonstrates significant beneficial relationships. The research included persons who self-identified as recovered but no longer met BPD criteria (recovered group) and those who did not self-identify as recovered but did meet BPD criteria (non-recovered group) (not recovered group). Age, ethnicity, and treatment history were often used to match people. As a result, 14 individual stories were incorporated (n = 7 recovered community and n = 7 not recoverable group).

5.3 Analyze data

Semi-structured interviews were conducted using a subject guide. After consulting with a customer advisory group, the material was amended to provide general interviewer instructions (Additional file 1). People were questioned about their initial encounters with BPD, current lifestyles, recovery perspectives, and care and support experiences. The interviews were recorded, transcribed verbatim, and evaluated using NVivo 11. Interpretive phenomenological analysis (IPA) was the general technique used to examine people's experiences, and the ascribed meaning associated with BPD rehabilitation was interpretive phenomenological analysis (IPA). For greater in-depth understanding, small sample numbers are advised. Colleagues and I used an inductive technique recommended by colleagues to characterize the emergent concepts and their relationships. To get a thorough understanding of the data, researchers began by immersing themselves in the story by reading transcripts and free coding. Second, unstructured data was recoded into emerging patterns that reflected bits and pieces of people's stories. Superordinate themes were devised to explain people's viewpoints on new concerns. Conversations inside the study team aided this technique, where consensus settled disagreements.

Two raters (FN and CM) categorized two transcripts that accounted for over 10% of the data independently (inter-rater reliability = 91%). One researcher coded the remaining data separately (FN). Respondents' identities have been de-identified to their respondent number due to privacy concerns. Those rescued are marked with an 'R,' while those who have not been marked with an 'NR.' The results were shared with a member of the user advisory committee once the researchers had agreed on the code. Their comments were included in the final report (MJ).

Findings

One hundred and seventy-one persons gave contact information for online survey follow-up, and 108 people were contacted. Thirty-nine people completed the telephone interview. The report comprised 14 human stories (7 recovered and seven not recovered) based on the study's inclusion criteria. The average age of the people in this sample was 33.36 years (SD = 10.26). The majority of the participants were from Australasia, with one from the Middle East. Between the two groups, there were no significant variations in socio-demographic characteristics.

5.4 Remission and Recovery from BPD

If you or someone you care about has been diagnosed with personality disorder (BPD), the first thing you'll ask is if it can be reversed. The good news is that BPD, which affects 1.4 percent of the US population, is treatable. 1. You'll be well on your way to recovery and remission in no time with the appropriate treatment.

Although "reversal" and "rehabilitation" do not indicate "cure," they do suggest that BPD has been adequately treated. Remission occurs when you no longer meet the criteria for a BPD diagnosis, as defined in the definition. The term "recovery" is more ambiguous, but it implies that you will devote a significant amount of time to improving all elements of your life. It includes things like keeping a career and having meaningful relationships.

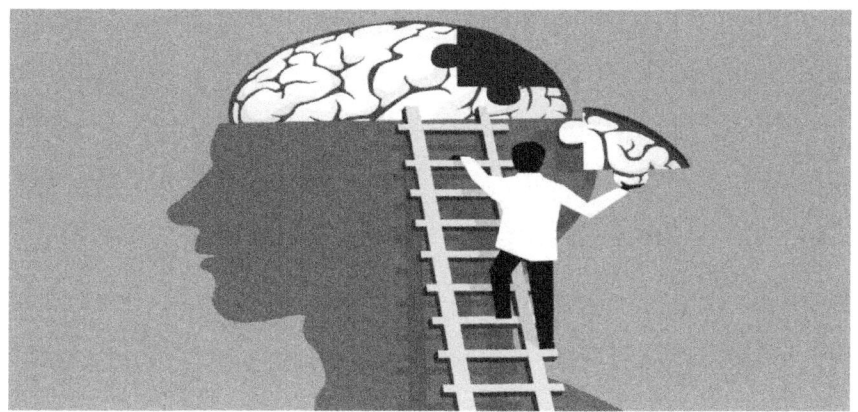

Treatment Objectives

BPD was thought to be incurable by most clinicians, who lumped it in with other difficult-to-treat diseases like psychopathy (ASPD). As scientists have learned more about the disorder, new treatment options have become available, allowing more people to achieve long-term recovery from BPD, usually via medication.

Because some people react differently than others, the results may vary. For the most part, BPD should be managed similarly to diabetes or other chronic diseases, with informed, tailored care. Although the sickness is unlikely to go away, it may improve one's quality of life.

Rates of Remission

According to 2015 research, by the time individuals reach adulthood, most persons with BPD will no longer fit the diagnostic criteria for the disorder. According to all accounts, many patients ultimately outgrow their symptoms and recover as the illness progresses. In a research published in 2012, 290 people with BPD were tracked for sixteen years, every two years. They discovered that recovery (defined as not satisfying the medical criteria for at least two years) seems to occur spontaneously after 2 to 8 years of diagnosis and treatment.

After 16 years, 99% of patients had attained a two-year remission, while 78% had reached an eight-year remission. The same research revealed that symptom relapses reduced with treatment, dropping from 36% after two years to roughly 10% after eight years. However, it's important to note that these figures only apply to those diagnosed with BPD and who have received treatment for it. The findings did not say what medication was provided or if alternative treatments were used. As a result, it's unclear how often different therapies affected remission rates or if misdiagnosed people may still recover.

Treatment Methodologies

The likelihood of complications or co-occurring disorders will impact how BPD is treated. Psychotherapy and drugs are often used to help people recover.

Psychotherapy

Psychotherapy, sometimes known as talk therapy, is the cornerstone treatment for BPD.

The following are some of the several methods:

- CBT (cognitive behavioral therapy) is a kind of talking therapy employed in all other types of psychotherapy.

- DBT is a kind of psychotherapy that focuses on identifying and changing negative thought patterns and giving skills for controlling emotions and dealing with anxiety.

- MBT (mentalization-based therapy) is a treatment that tries to improve people's ability to think clearly.

- SFT is a kind of psychotherapy that focuses on identifying and changing deeply ingrained thinking and behavior patterns from our past.

- Transference-focused therapy (TFT) is psychotherapy that seeks to prevent negative sentiments about past events and individuals from transferring to present circumstances.

STEPPS (Systems programming for cognitive predictability and problem solving) is a 20-week educational program that teaches persons with BPD how to recognize the habits and feelings associated with their condition and modify their behaviors and regulate their emotions.

Both therapies effectively treat BPD, but they take distinct approaches to the disorder. There isn't one that is fundamentally superior to the others. The method you choose is mostly determined by the efficiency of your past meetings with your psychiatrist and your willingness to try it.

Never be afraid to inquire why your doctor favors a certain psychological method. It will assist you in better understanding the treatment's goals and determining if it is the best choice.

Prescription drugs

Any of the symptoms of BPD may be treated with medication. 5 While not all medications are necessary, the following are some of the most often prescribed: Antidepressants such as selective serotonin reuptake inhibitors (SSRIs) are often used as first-line treatment for depression. Antipsychotic drugs like Zyprexa (olanzapine) help people with BPD manage their impulsivity, aggressiveness, and depressive symptoms.

Mood stabilisers such as topiramate (topiramate), lamotrigine (lamotrigine), and valproate semi sodium (Depakote) may help moderate BPD violence. Ativan (lorazepam), Klonopin (clonazepam), Xanax (alprazolam), and Valium (Valium) are anti-anxiety drugs (diazepam)

Co-Occurring Disorders

According to the National Institute of Mental Health (NIMH), 85 percent of BPD also experience anxiety, impulse control challenges, alcohol abuse or addiction disorders, or mental diseases (like major depressive disorder or MDD). People with BPD might also be diagnosed with a variety of other behavioral disorders. Three of the most common co-occurring symptoms in BPD are listed below. Due to overlapping effects, co-occurring disorders (comorbidities) may make a recovery more challenging and lead to missing or delayed diagnoses.

When a dual diagnosis is obtained, it's usual to order treatment such that the condition with the best chance of improvement is treated first. If you have MDD, comorbidity like BPD, an antidepressant may be recommended to help with the depressive symptoms that both MDD and BPD cause.

Adapting

There are things you can do to help yourself survive while seeking therapy, whether you suspect you have BPD or have been diagnosed. Please do not be alarmed. Keep in mind that you have a strong possibility of recovering. Early detection and therapy usually provide better outcomes than later diagnosis and treatment in other mental health diseases.

Seek out professionals who have dealt with BPD before. It not only reduces the risk of delayed diagnosis and comorbidities, but it also increases the chances of obtaining far more up-to-date treatment with the fewest possible side effects and issues.

Chapter 6: How to help yourself if you had a BPD?

Mental anguish, impulsivity, relationship issues, and substantial stress-related behavioral changes are all symptoms of BPD. BPD has a significant influence on seeing yourself and interacting with others. It may also find it challenging to react to stressful events effectively. People with BPD may find it challenging to hold a job or establish solid relationships with others due to their symptoms.

A trained medical professional can only detect BPD. Psychotherapy is typically the first line of defense against BPD symptoms; however, your "doctor" may also recommend medication, and both are successful in lowering BPD symptoms. If you desire extra assistance, these self-help approaches should be combined with medicine.

6.1 Self-Help for Borderline Personality Disorder

Educate Yourself

It's crucial to comprehend the implications of a BPD diagnosis. It might include learning about the symptoms of your disease so you can recognize and address them sooner, as well as knowing your doctor's treatment plan so you can identify areas of your life where you could need additional help. Many professional BPD therapies have an educational component and reading "BPD" education has been shown to help symptoms.

You may learn more about your condition in a variety of ways. The first step during the BPD evaluation phase is to ask your therapist for further information. Questions to think about include (but are not limited to):

- Why do you have "BPD" symptoms?

- What impact would they have on your career and personal relationships?

- Is it conceivable that, in addition to BPD, you have additional mental health issues?

- What did you do to make your condition worse?

- What does your rehabilitation strategy entail?

- Is it required that you take medication?

- How long will you be undergoing therapy for BPD?

- What would you do if you were treating my symptoms at home?

In general, you should feel free to ask your psychiatrist any questions you have at any time throughout your appointment. All of this is part of establishing a solid therapeutic connection that will benefit the patient in the long run.

Grounding yourself

Seeking help from a close friend or family member Learning great coping skills like "engaged listening," "viewing things from another person's perspective," and "relying entirely on the present scenario" may be beneficial for those with BPD who struggle with relationships.

Emotional Expression

Because BPD is often connected with strong emotions like rage, many BPD people avoid expressing their feelings. On the other hand, suppressing your thoughts will not make them go away and may instead cause you to become more focused on the sentiments you're attempting to overcome.

Instead, think about finding healthy outlets for your feelings. Some individuals express themselves by keeping a book or diary, while others paint or draw, and still, others express themselves by dancing, singing, or playing music. Increased physical well-being and a reduction in depressive symptoms may be two of the advantages of expressive literature.

Using these approaches might be unpleasant or even distressing for some individuals. Discuss any worries you have about expressing your feelings with your psychiatrist. They'll assist you in determining which activities, if any, are a good match for you.

Mindfulness

Mindfulness may be especially beneficial for those with "BPD." Mindfulness enables you to be more aware of your feelings, emotions, and sensations, which might help you recognize when your signs (symptoms) are becoming worse. Mindfulness "meditation" is a systematic kind of mindfulness practice that has been shown in trials to assist patients with BPD in managing their symptoms. Mindfulness therapy is a multitasking self-help strategy that may assist people with BPD overcome depression.

Mindfulness is a technique that encourages people to live more "in the now" rather than worrying about the future, the past, or our thoughts. It also entails paying attention to what's happening around you and your emotions without being too critical, cynical, or contemplative.

For many of us, mindfulness is notoriously elusive, requiring a considerable deal of meditation and careful analysis. This "state of mind" may be achieved via yoga and other relaxing techniques. On the other hand, mindfulness may assist persons with "mental illnesses in general, and BPD in particular" in achieving serenity and minimizing symptoms. Coloring with pencils or stickers, for example, may be a simple approach for some individuals to practice mindfulness. Mindfulness is also a crucial component of dialectical behavior therapy, which has been demonstrated to be effective in treating BPD.

Identify Diagnostic Tools

You won't identify yourself or a loved one with BPD since you're a mental health professional. A medical practitioner can only make the diagnosis. In any event, the internet has made taking standardized tests to determine whether or not you have a borderline personality disorder much easier. Other testing choices may be found by Googling "internet depression assessment" or "online anxiety evaluation," and I suggest Dr. Kristin Neff's online self-compassion exam.

These strategies can help you understand more about yourself and your symptoms, even if they aren't ideal. Only test if it is reliable and was developed using cutting-edge research and medical practices. This essay about the benefits and drawbacks of self-diagnosing may also be interesting.

Meditation

People with a borderline personality disorder may benefit from meditation, often known as mindfulness. Meditation and awareness are intricately intertwined.

Meditation provides several advantages. Meditation strategies for calming the mind include slowing down, focusing on emotions, breathing, and chanting. Meditations come in various forms, each with its own set of benefits.

Numerous studies have shown the positive effects of "meditation" on overall mental health. Reducing anxiety and depression symptoms will help patients feel more at ease and home. This will (in actuality) help people have happier interactions, manage emotional tension, and regulate emotional outbursts, all of which may have a big influence on people with BPD. According to a clinical study, people with BPD who meditate daily see improvements in various symptoms.

Podcasts

Most individuals who listen to podcasts regularly know that each episode teaches them something new. Podcasts on healthy relationships, yoga, self-care, and dealing with stress and sadness are available. There's a podcast for you to listen to if you're interested.

Distract Yourself

When you're in a bind, the only thing you can do is divert your attention away from the source of your distress. It isn't going to be simple, but practice makes perfect. What would you do if you needed to be diverted from your work? Fortunately, there are several options.

What do you prefer to do when you have free time? Would you want to learn how to knit? Are you a fan of a good challenge? Do you want to sketch something? What should you do if you want to write something? Look for a project that interests you and get straight in.

Are there any tasks around the home or at work that you could do?

It is a difficult distraction. It might be very uncomfortable and almost impossible to complete. It will take some time to find out how to divert your attention and which activity and strategy will be most effective for you. The most important thing is that you give it your best. You could discover that indulging in a hobby is the most effective way to get through a crisis or a period of significant mental discomfort. If you reevaluate after some time has passed and have finished their duties, that would be fantastic. However, forcing oneself into a difficult situation to improve one's situation is often the key.

DBT Skills Training

DBT (dialectical behavior therapy) is a scientifically validated practice that has helped people all across the country preserve their lives. Unfortunately, DBT is either unavailable or too expensive in many parts of the globe. If you don't have a therapist and are on the DBT waiting list, online skills training may be a good approach to gain the skills you need.

- Through online skill testing, you'll learn how to control your emotions and urges, as well as how to relieve (yourself) when you're angry.

- Here's how to be a happier, healthier version of yourself, whether you're bored, empty, or even self-destructive.

Seek Online Support

One of the most major advantages of the modern period in which we live is that there is no assistance for those in need. Individuals searching for help and information may find it on various Facebook groups and online sites. On Twitter, the hashtag #BPDChat has been suggested. Many people seeking communication and inspiration would find it an exciting and hopeful resource.

These programs may assist you in expressing your thoughts, addressing coping strategies, and meeting loving and validating individuals, among other things. Please keep in mind that you are not alone and that you may be able to meet someone with whom you can share your healing and hope stories.

On the other hand, online therapy should not be mistaken for medical treatment from a trained professional. While some online forums are helpful and encouraging places to get help and information, others may include false or dangerous information.

6.2 Self-care for BPD

You must participate in the healing process to recover. The activities you should do are as follows:

- Make a plan to cope with your BPD with the help of your healthcare provider (and, if possible, your wife or family).

- Keep track of your meetings and arrive on time.

- Any concerns you may have should be handled with your caregiver.

- Allow them to assist you in making alterations to your everyday routine and decisions.

- You must complete all chores or "homework" as part of your mental therapy.

- Telling the truth about your bipolar condition is the best thing you can do. Consider the situation again to understand the crisis or what causes you to injure yourself.

- Gain a greater understanding of dealing with your emotions, desires, and relationships. Instead of damaging yourself, learn to live with it.

- Continue to work hard until you regain control of your life and mental health.

- Get the right information. All information is welcome. The information regarding BPD available on the "internet" is inaccurate. Consult your doctor about BPD therapy and rehabilitation (or another competent therapist).

- Make a safety plan to help you get through difficult times.

Coping with the Bad times

You may get upset when something seems to be too tough for you to handle. The word "crisis" is used to characterize this circumstance.

When you see the doctor amid a disaster, they will be more concerned with the 'here and now.' It's probably not the greatest moment to start a long conversation on personal experiences or friendship issues. It's typically best to address such concerns later in your primary care physician's standard treatment.

Despite your intense emotions, you should remain driven to discover answers to your difficulties, which means the BPD treatment team will not make any of your choices for you. They will solicit your feedback and expect you to participate in creating a rehabilitation program.

Planning to keep "yourself" safe.

Make a plan for what you'll do if you find yourself in an emergency, including what you'll do to be safe and when to call 911. A protection plan is another name for this kind of plan. Having a defensive strategy in place might help you think more clearly when you're upset. You may make a strategy with the aid of your healthcare practitioner that you will keep to until you feel better. You may also provide a copy to your wife (partner) or other family members.

Request that the primary health care physician who supervises the BPD collaborate with you to develop a safety plan. It should be considered separately from the rest of the management strategy.

Resources that will help you plan are (available) from:

- Beyond the pale of blue

- Air Strategy Project

- A world leader in personality disorder research, education, and treatment.

Information that must be in the safety plan

- Your treatment and problem-solving objectives, as well as a list of short- and long-term objectives.

- Situations that make you feel terrified or enraged to the point of putting your life in jeopardy.

- Things you should do to survive a disaster – this might include strategies you've used in the past that have helped you survive and aren't harmful.

- What not to do in a crisis - make a list of things you've done in the past that either didn't work or worsened the situation.

- Things your wife or family will help you and make life easier for you.

- Make a list of people who know you (for example, your wife or a relative, your therapist, school counselor, caseworker, or general practitioner), as well as organizations that may be able to assist you in a crisis (e.g., Lifeline, a mental health line, emergency services).

Psychoeducation

Psychoeducation is a method of educating persons with "BPD" (and their partners or family members) about the condition. Symptoms, therapy, coping skills, and institutions that may assist are all covered in psychoeducation classes. Psychoeducation should be utilized in tandem with standard psychiatric care.

Psychoeducation may be done one-on-one or in a group setting. Written materials, recordings, blogs, seminars, and consultations with the therapist or another qualified mental health expert are just a few examples.

Check with your doctor to see if any local services are available.

Support that includes families

Your loved ones will assist you in comprehending your condition and learning how to comfort you while you recover. If at all possible, include your family in your management strategy. Make a list of everyone from your family or friends that the care expert will speak with and make a note of it.

It will be better for you and your family if you and your family discuss the full facts of your diagnosis and recovery options. If you and your partner communicate effectively, you'll be able to work toward the same therapeutic objective.

Family psychoeducation programs aid communication and problem-solving. Family psychoeducation benefits all members of the family. It's terrible to see a loved one acquire BPD.

You may get a copy of your medical records to show your family or girlfriend (including prescription & psychiatric treatment).

What if one has kids?

Even though BPD makes parenting difficult, you can always be a good parent. The most important thing you can do (for your children) is to keep working on "your" therapy to improve and protect them from the impacts of BPD as soon as feasible. A parenting program may help you learn new skills if you believe you might assist with parenting. Consult a doctor or another medical expert for assistance. If you have a kid, you can keep them with you even if you need to go to hospital.

6.3 5 Ways to Make the Most of The BPD Treatment

The most common treatment for borderline personality disorder is psychotherapy, sometimes known as "talk therapy."

In patients with bipolar illness, BPD conversation therapy aims to improve functioning, control emotions, and reduce impulsivity.

DBT is one of the methods used to treat BPD (Dialectical Behavior Therapy). DBT is a therapy that incorporates both social and individual therapy. Patients are taught strategies to control their emotions better, cope with stress, and strengthen their relationships. Teletherapy and video consultation may also be used to treat BPD.

The FDA has not approved any BPD medications (Food and Drug Administration). In addition, medications for diseases or co-occurring "mental health disorders" may be provided. Antidepressants and mood stabilizers are two medications that may help persons with BPD.

While counseling for BPD may be the first step (toward) successful treatment, there are other options for BPD management:

1. Be the "Active Part" for Your Treatment Plan

You must seek treatment for borderline personality disorder, and you should make every effort to be an active, involved participant in the program you've chosen. As you gain more knowledge, you'll be better able to ask pertinent questions, make comments, and communicate with care professionals openly and honestly. There is no one-size-fits-all therapy for BPD. It will take time to get everything in order.

2. Try some Grounding Exercises

Grounding activities might assist you in learning to manage BPT symptoms. The only goal of the grounding exercises is to help you concentrate your attention on the present moment. The idea is to focus on what is going on right now rather than what has occurred in the "past" or what will happen in the future.

Various types of "grounding exercises":

- Visual and auditory grounding exercises are used in visual and aural activities to bring you back to the present moment. Take time to look around before you begin your visual activities. Take a look at what you've seen. Make an effort to pay attention to the little things. Following the "same steps" as a (visual) grounding exercise, you may get the same result with sounds in an auditory exercise. Make an effort to pick up on even the tiniest sounds and the distinctions between them. Visual and "auditory grounding" are great since they may be done anyplace, and no one will notice.

- Tactile activities to help you feel more grounded. Tactile grounding exercises are ways to use your sense of touch to bring yourself into the present moment. Various approaches may be used to accomplish this. Taking a cold shower, for example, may be beneficial. Wearing a "rubber band" around your wrist and gently snapping it may improve your awareness of your surroundings.

- Using a therapy instrument to help you relax. You may use several meditation applications to help you focus your thoughts and return to a more precise level of awareness. Examine your phone's software to find the greatest match for you. Using a guided treatment program for a few minutes each day will help you remain focused.

- Aromatherapy is the use of essential oils to treat a variety of ailments. When you're experiencing a dissociative episode or displaying signs of BPD, aromatherapy using essential oils may help you remain present and calm. Look for lavender or chamomile scents.

- It is beneficial to exercise the lungs. Learn to take long, deep breaths through your nose until you can no longer take any more. Then thoroughly evacuate the air from your lungs using your teeth. Repetition and concentration on the sensations of extending and then compressing the lungs.

- It's wise to try out a few different grounding techniques before deciding on one that works for you.

3. Get the Emergency Safety Plan

The emotional torment you suffer due to "BPD" is one of the most difficult aspects of the condition. It might result in a mental health emergency. You could, for example, have "suicidal thoughts" or activities. Make an emergency safety plan when you're thinking clearly and in a good mood. Make a plan for what you'll do if you think you're endangering yourself or others.

Make a comprehensive plan so that you won't be able to think as clearly in a potentially dangerous situation as you were while you were preparing the plan.

4. Get Support

You will isolate yourself if you have "BPD." You may be feeling alone because you're having relationship issues and are afraid of being judged. It's crucial to have a reliable and trustworthy social support network, such as friends or family, in place.

To build connections, consider forming a community group for people with BPD.

5. Practice "Self-Care."

Physical and mental health are intertwined. Physical activity may also assist you in better managing your BPD. Eating a good diet, exercising frequently, and getting adequate sleep are all examples of self-care. Discover entertaining ways to unwind and de-stress. Make a timetable and a habit that permits you to engage in your favorite pastimes.

Overcoming "BPD" Without Medication

Even though it is possible to overcome BPD without medication, you should seek the advice and recovery plan of your doctor or health care provider. When it comes to BPD, medication isn't necessarily the first line of defense. It is mostly used to treat serious disorders such as depression and mood swings.

Whether or not you can take medication for "BPD," you should learn coping skills and lead a healthy lifestyle rather than allowing the condition and its effects to define you.

It's vital to develop tactics that appeal to you and change your mindset from pessimism to optimism. You may even wish to inform your family and friends of your needs. Allow family members to know how to "help" you, for example, when you're furious or agitated. Loved ones will want to cheer you up and assist you, but they won't know-how.

Chapter 7: How the "BPD" affects families

A growing body of "empirical" research on families and BPD (borderline personality disorder). Studies of childhood trauma perpetrated by family members (e.g., physical, emotional, and sexual abuse, witnessing violence) and hereditary influences on affected people's temperamental features are a big element of this research. However, in this issue of The Interface, we've chosen to concentrate on the growing amount of research on psychopathology in BPD families, as well as the more recent subject of family care.

Psychopathology in extended families in BPD patients. Various psychopathological traits in large families of BPD probands were compared to large families of a placebo proband in various tests. Silverman and colleagues, for example, examined the first-degree relatives of three proband subsamples: those with BPD, other personality disorders, and schizophrenia. Families of BPD probands had greater affective and impulsive issues than the other two subsamples. A report on family members with medical probands on the borderline and non-borderline. People with BPD have considerably higher rates of despair, drug misuse, and antisocial behavior in their communities. People with BPD are more prone than those who have never been psychiatrically unwell to experience mood disorders. Researchers found that BPD probands' families had more mood and Axis II issues than the two control groups. Family members with (341) BPD probands were compared to 104 with another form of Axis II disorder in a large sample. A total of 1500 BPD patients' relatives were questioned. BPD Families' "probands" are more likely than non-BPD Axis II probands to have BPD subsyndromal symptoms, especially psychopathology symptoms. Finally, White et al. examined their study of the "literature" on psychopathology in relatives of people with BPD (2003) review paper. This author group concluded that there are no apparent ancestors of schizophrenia and depression but BPD and impulse control disorders. What conclusions can we draw from this collection of research on the psychopathology of BPD relatives? These findings consistently reveal a relationship between four categories of family psychopathology: (1) mood disorders, (2) response disorders, (3) alcohol use disorders, and (4) BPD-related Axis-II problems.

The probands' psychopathology seems to be mirrored in the family of BPD patients.

7.1 borderline personality disorder (BPD) & Your Family

Stress on Family

Family members may be distressed by seeing a loved one suffer from BPD and coping with the unpleasant relationship symptoms of BPD. When a loved one with BPD engages in self-destructive activities, family members may feel powerless. It is especially true for parents and guardians of teenagers with BPD who may become erratic. Many members of the "BPD" family may suffer great psychological agony due to any of the high-risk behaviors associated with BPD, in addition to the ongoing hardship of caring for a loved one with BPD. People with BPD are more likely to engage in self-harming activities such as cutting and burning. These habits might swiftly spiral out of control, leading to accidental fatality. Additionally, those with "BPD" have a greater risk of suicide.

As a result of dealing with high-risk activities (such as rushing a loved one to the hospital after an attempted suicide), family members may suffer psychological distress (which may develop to significant issues like "post-traumatic stress disorder" in extreme instances).

Guilt & Responsibility

Many "BPD" family members describe their embarrassment as difficult. Studies on BPD etiology link "childhood maltreatment" such as neglect or violence to BPD development. There's also a strong genetic component. They feel guilty or ashamed even if they did not affect their loved one's BPD development.

Like many family members, many are confused about their involvement in their loved one's rehabilitation.

Some families want to be hopeful, but they fear fostering "BPD-related" behaviors like self-harm. Others want to help but are irritated by the BPD's behavior. Finally, some people struggle to sympathize due to "psychiatric" concerns. A family history of BPD may affect other family members.

Struggles Families Experience

Managing a loved one's medication adds to the challenges of BPD. Many specialists and teams, as well as various stages of therapy (including partial / inpatient hospitalization and outpatient treatment), are available to the "BPD family."

For example, is your loved one's demeanor softer than normal, or have they stopped taking their meds as prescribed?), give transportation to appointments, or organize the search for new treatment choices. It's not easy navigating these realities and the greater mental health setting, which may add to a family's BPD struggles.

Broader Effects

Unfortunately, having a family member with "BPD" may cause stress, challenges, and concerns with assistance for both direct and extended family members. Parents of adolescents and adults with BPD emphasize the significant strain that is merely caring for a child with BPD can have on a marriage. This kind of stress is frequent in couples, leading to divorce or breakup.

Siblings are also influenced in a variety of ways. Others may withdraw from the family to protect themselves (or their spouses, children, or other family members) or escape the emotional suffering of being close to someone with BPD.

The BPD family support system includes grandparents, aunts, uncles, and other friends who understand how difficult it is to care for someone with BPD.

Getting Help

It might be difficult for family members to get the help and support they need to care for a loved one who has "BPD." There are options and services available if you're serious about receiving treatment. To begin, if you feel your loved one is suffering from BPD and they have not sought therapy, urge them to do so.

Dealing with "mental health system."

The aggravation of not receiving timely and trustworthy therapy adds to the family's stress. Clinicians also rely on families to help with service coordination, which may include many clinicians and teams and various stages of treatment ranging from frequent visits to brief hospitalizations.

Family members must monitor their loved one's mental and physical well-being, provide transportation to appointments, and coordinate the search for new solutions. Navigating the "mental health system" to find the appropriate solution is a challenging endeavor that adds to the family's stress.

Effects on the family relationships

Parents of adolescents and adults with BPD report how caring for their children may burden their marriage, resulting in divorce or breakup.

Siblings of children with BPD parents may be forced to become guardians, while others may avoid intimate contact with persons with BPD to avoid emotional suffering. Grandparents, aunts, uncles, and other relatives in the BPD family support network may feel the pressure of caring for a person with BPD.

7.2 Experiences

Unaware of BPD, it is a personality condition characterized by a "jack of all trades" approach. People with the disease have trouble controlling their impulses, managing their emotions, and deciding what they want to be in life (identity the confusion). They don't have to be insane to misunderstand even the most innocent-sounding unfavorable remarks. They cut, smoke, and harm themselves sometimes. They make "suicide threats" and have anger management difficulties. They mistrust people and tend to "zone out" or detach when pressed.

Psychiatrists say they break people into two categories: deities and rubbish heaps. Doctors typically characterize BPD patients as adept manipulators. Manipulators may be unable to assess a person's strengths and defects simultaneously. Simply, they couldn't. It's typically just a ploy to make the patient's parents seem awful.

Their behavior is sometimes so odd that it's easy to think they're insane. However, other therapists dispute that BPD is a disorder rather than a collection of unpleasant personality traits that develop in certain children from problematic households.

Why do they assert this? For two reasons. Many other "therapists" who encounter BPD patients independently developed the same strategies. Patients with BPD, like a faucet, may turn any of their symptoms on or off at will. [Many readers have emphasized that I mean mental symptoms, not how they feel on the inside.] Patients with serious mental illnesses like schizophrenia or melancholic depression, I believe, cannot. Second, when the truth about their background is revealed, virtually all individuals come from families with serious familial pathology.

Many studies show that child abuse and neglect are the most frequent biological, psychological, and social risk factors among those with the disorder. Notably, not all maltreated or abandoned children develop BPD, and many BPD patients have never been sexually or physically molested.

It's a how-to guide for developing BPD patients without injuring them. Contrasting parental signals are the most common cause of borderline conduct in children.

The main issue with "borderline" families is that their "parents" see their function as parents as the be-all and end-all of human life. Regardless, they despise being parents and consider their kids as a burden.

It's OK to blame someone's behavior on parental issues, but it pushes the causation question back a decade. This chapter focuses on one or more children in certain households, leaving the others unaffected.

Disagreements between parents regarding the role of "father" lead to animosity (over-involvement) and antagonism (under-involvement) with or without violence.

The youngsters understand their parents' "message," which means "I need you." But I hate you because this sequence implies a double message." Waiting long enough will bring the opposite extreme of over-involvement or under-involvement.

To restore family harmony, the infant must "answer" the following "question": How can they be a crucial part of their lives (even if communication is limited) while still offering a clear rationale and outlet for their anger? The Spoiler function is the ideal solution, and it's fantastic.

Therapist Melanie Klein was the first to identify spoiling as a "child's primitive" jealousy of their mother's breasts. The idea was virtually "insane," yet she articulated a very likely adult behavior pattern.

In short, the spoiler kid refuses to develop, stays reliant on the parent, and wrecks and debases all their parents want for them. When a female child mistreats or loses expensive designer clothing, she demands replacements and more "mother's time."

There is no right or wrong way to parent. They will symbolically pee on everything their parents do for them, even as adults. Parents are often accused of being arrogant, bossy, uninformed, or cruel. They are obliviously detested. The way parents are treated invalidating.

Psychiatrist Marsha Linehan believes that an "invalidating environment" paired with a genetic propensity to be overly emotional is one of the two key causes of BPD. She doesn't say where, but it's presumably the "person's" family.

Disagreeing with someone's position does not invalidate them. Someone suggests the target's thoughts and sentiments are invalid, illogical, selfish, insensitive, uninformed, and maybe mad. The target's feelings are wrong. Invalidators make it clear to their targets that their thoughts and views are irrelevant at any moment and in any form. In some families, validation leads to physical violence and even murder. However, linguistic manipulations that are rejected in subtle and perplexing ways may invalidate. Invalidation of the infant by the parents is common in BPD homes. After a while, the infant begins acting as the boy did to his parents. They begin to give and receive.

Spoiled children and adults will never live independently of their parents. As a consequence, the parents appear to be smitten with their kids. Paradoxically, the child's outrageous conduct allows the parents to express their often-silent disdain for their children.

Parents blame themselves for their failures as parents, adding to their uneasiness. So, the infant may attempt to "control" their inclinations. Anger makes parents' kids embarrassed. If they are guilty, the youngster is upset.

Practicing the spoiler stance with others is required because of its difficulty. And, of course, psychiatrists. Nobody else will tolerate them for long.

Remember that a BPD adult frequently chooses to be the spoiler, so their behaviors can't be entirely blamed on their parents. BPD patients "After a point, they give as good as they get.

7.3 Family members' experiences with a parent diagnosed with BPD.

Background

The researcher saw the therapeutic benefits of mindfulness therapy offered to people with BPD while working at a mental facility. Family members who attempted to assist their BPD-affected loved ones received no assistance. There was a lot of tension, anguish, sorrow, and loneliness among the family members.

Objectives

The goal of this study was to understand more about and explain the connections amongst family members who have a loved one with BPD.

Method

The study was conducted using a qualitative, exploratory, descriptive, and contextual study technique. A random survey of family members ranging in age from 24 to 74 was undertaken. Eight in-depth "phenomenological" interviews, as well as field notes, were done. "Tell me about getting a parent diagnosed with BPD" was the major theme of the interviews. An impartial coder checked the data before meeting with the "researcher" for a consensus evaluation of the findings. There were safeguards in place to ensure trustworthiness and adherence to ethical standards.

Results

There were four primary patterns discovered. Family members spoke about their BPD-diagnosed relative's mental, physical, interpersonal, and self-dysregulation issues in subject one. Family members endured social shame, financial pressure, and marital strife due to their bad feelings against their relatives. They felt obligated to develop and enhance their mental health in these two. Family members in these three cases had to go through a difficult adjustment and coping process. Family members were on the lookout for peace and integration in theme four.

Conclusion

According to the findings, family members felt powerless since they were unaware of their relative's BPD. Mental health experts and caregivers are currently researching BPD, it's meaning and implications, and treatment and care choices.

Discussion of findings

Family members with BPD have physical, cognitive, behavioral, interpersonal, and self-regulation issues.

Families with BPD showed dysregulation, causing chaos and instability in the home. In our study, relatives with BPD had difficulty regulating their emotions. Problems detecting or feeling emotions result from relationship difficulties. The inability to adjust or recognize aspects of one's "emotional" experience. They are very "emotionally" aroused, limiting their capacity to act.

Cognitive dysregulation caused (perceived) estrangement in BPD relatives. The research found that relatives are sensitive to criticism and judgment and feel unsupported by their family members. Conversations that make sense to other family members are typically viewed negatively by BPD relatives.

Situations that upset BPD families caused behavioral dysregulation. It resulted in dangerous behaviors, including drug and opiate addiction, cutting, unhealthy sexual practices, and suicidality. An incorrect response may cause a family member to lash out, endangering their lives. BPD causes impulsivity. Self-injury, opiate usage, casual sex with strangers, and reckless driving are the most harmful behaviors. Originally, these behaviors were used to control and lessen emotional intensity.

Depressive relationships typically stem from interpersonal dysregulation. Also, families are unaware of their relatives' erratic behavior. These activities cause family discord and rifts. BPD relatives fear being abandoned by those who matter most in their lives. Their former relationships appear marked by discord, ambivalence, frustration, melancholy, and emptiness. Troubled marriages are tough to manage and sustain.

Psychopathology was defined as a person's incapacity to see their strengths. Family members of BPD patients couldn't establish a sense of self. People and surroundings affected how they felt. It led to inappropriate behavior and unhealthy relationships. Families with BPD couldn't seek help from relatives. Identity changes such as loss of self-identity and poor self-acceptance were self-dysregulation symptoms revealed by BPD relatives. BPD relatives struggle to build a sense of self and see themselves as entire beings. Their views, desires, identities, and self-perceptions shift.

The inner- and behavioral interactions of members of the family who have been diagnosed with BPD.

Family members who had BPD experienced unpleasant responses. Distress, grief, and regret were among the emotions felt.

Families with BPD suffered despair due to internal stress and catastrophes. The bonds between family members were tested. BPD family members have mocked and dismissed their relatives' worries.

The unpredictable, out-of-control behavior of BPD relatives has been shown to harm family members. Family members frequently feel alienated due to their BPD relative's urge to eliminate relationships. Also humiliated were relatives. Anxious and disruptive relatives with BPD were more prone to act out. Family members of BPD sufferers feel ridiculed and unable to cope with their relative's behavior.

Discuss how family members avoid BPD-affected relatives, causing tension, guilt, and shame. Stigmatization causes a social and emotional burden on family members. As a consequence, they demand less government assistance. Family members may feel guilty and humiliated. They blame their relative's troubles. Stigmatized people may feel displaced, alone, and discriminated against. Social withdrawal occurs when family members fear exclusion, resulting in diminished social support networks.

This research showed how their relatives' immoral behavior harmed their finances. Family members pay for hospitalization, opioid or alcohol therapy, inpatient psychiatric treatment, and other expenditures. Parents of "female" BPD children have been financially harmed in several ways. Insufficient compliance with treatment centers and other facilities by relatives diagnosed with BPD, financial difficulties, anxiety about the relative's prospects, and displeasure with the relative's care and rehabilitation were commonly stated by relatives' families.

Extra stress and unresolved domestic trauma lead to marital strife. Caring for someone with a "personality problem" causes stress, worry, and alienation among family members and peers.

High-stress levels in marriages may lead to rifts and, finally, divorce.

Family members went through a difficult adaptation & coping mechanism.

Family disputes and quarrels led to inadequate coping techniques. Family members felt disempowered due to their inability to govern their lives. Medical services were available but underfunded and overloaded. There was a lack of information to help family members cope with BPD-affected families. Family members think they can't safeguard a (relative) with BPD and are reluctant to assist. Mental illness is as contagious as the flu or tuberculosis.

Ineffective coping mechanisms are linked to poor communication and understanding among "family members" of BPD patients. The health sector could not satisfy patient requirements due to a lack of knowledge of BPD. Due to a lack of expertise, several doctors refused to treat BPD patients. For unclear reasons, BPD relatives may separate themselves from family members. Families report that BPD patients are seldom taught impulse control in programs and residential care.

Poor coping skills were often linked to inexperienced family members. Thus, making the best options for their BPD-affected families was difficult.

Members of the family were on a mission for harmony & integration.

Family members choose to reconnect with BPD loved ones and change their caregiving methods. Family members want autonomy, self-determination, trust, care, and self-maintenance. So, they took charge of their health.

After taking part in this study, relatives of BPD patients said they felt better about their jobs as caregivers. They gained inner strength and professional success by being positive and willing to take risks. Family members must direct their growth.

Family members wanted to restore trust and caring. They learned new skills and appreciated the group's help. They learned what worked and what didn't. A few genuine and scientifically confirmed BPD books may be helpful to family members.

Family members must be self-caring to aid their BPD relatives properly. The family learned to laugh at themselves and not take themselves too seriously. Family members get a sense of self.

Help from professionals and neighbors is common. Until recently, Australian mental health providers undervalued the importance of treating and caring for BPD patients. Many people were refused treatment because they were deemed difficult, bothersome, and helpless. Family members have no idea how to care for a person with BPD.

Chapter 8: How family & friends can help?

Support of family

To say your family relationships were put to the test many years before you were diagnosed. Your inability to deal with or comprehend your powerful emotions exacerbated family problems; you responded angrily and mentally, unable to cope with or comprehend your high feelings.

Your parents are both quite knowledgeable about the sickness, even though it took them a long time to get so. Your mother may have sought assistance at the Vancouver "Dialectical Behavior Therapy" Centre before you accepted treatment, where she learned about "BPD" and gained some skills to help her (as a parent) with a child with the condition. Your father has learned much more about mental health concerns. He is now the most ardent supporter in your attempts to eliminate stigma and raise awareness of BPD among the general population. It's difficult for your parents to know what to do when you're in a difficult situation. If you seek assistance, such as going to the (hospital) emergency room, they will try their utmost to assist you, even if they don't completely comprehend what's going on.

Some family members who have been affected by your illness may take longer to heal until they can forgive what occurred in the years leading up to your treatment. Family and friends find it difficult to watch you seem to be in a perpetual state of crisis, with apparently random "outbursts" of verbal and physical aggression, ups and downs in your relationships with others, and suicidality producing concern in those around you. Many individuals who have known you for a long time may have seen changes in your conduct due to the event. Counseling programs will educate you on better control your emotions, healthily cope with stress, and interact with others. As a result, your family and friends have gotten closer to you. Talking about the condition may help you understand why some of your behavior and feelings are the way they are, and it can also help you forecast prospective difficulties.

Support of friends

You may have concealed your sickness for a long time because you were terrified of it, only informing those who needed to know. You may start telling your "friends" what's going on after completing a dialectical behavior therapy course in January 2015 and feeling happier and more stable on your own. BPD is a relatively unknown illness, and your peers have no idea what it is. They were, however, excellent at asking nonjudgmental questions and doing research to have a better understanding of what was going on in your life.

All of your friends are like family to you, and they are your most ardent advocates. In addition to keeping, you happy and amused regularly and making you feel loved, they've taught you how to cope with problems when they happen. You may have spent the majority of your time since finishing the treatment course delighted, busy, and in control of your "emotions." There will, however, be days when you are in a panic (although these crisis periods are few & far between & much less "intense" than they used to be before treatment). You may not remember talking about what to do in a crisis with your friends, but they all seemed to know "how to help."

People went through a lengthy period of crisis due to a bad combination of burnout, a medication change that didn't work for me, and some social stressors. Your crises usually last a few hours or days, but this time they lasted over a month, replete with suicidality, self-harming desires, and a sense of dread.

Your friends raced to your rescue as soon as they realized anything was wrong (less than 24 hours after starting to withdraw from college, feeling hopeless, & becoming increasingly suicidal). One of them called and invited you to stay with them for the weekend since you "needed a pal." It was an attractive invitation: you came over, sat in front of the television, laughed, and ate together. In your opinion, this is the greatest way to keep your friends and family safe when they are in danger. You don't have to say anything; all you have to do is show there, keep them occupied, and make sure they're safe.

The pals are fantastic in calming you down. They will never forsake you, never let you reschedule arrangements, and never make you feel uncomfortable throughout that month. Every day, they checked in on you, making sure you were "going out the door" and listening to your ideas anytime you wanted.

8.1 How can you help when the ones you care for are in danger?

Untreated BPD may lead to a host of issues for both the person with BPD and their family and friends. Accepting family and friends' love and aiding persons with "BPD" during a crisis may be challenging owing to the disorder's emphasis on interpersonal ties. What has been found is as follows:

- It's critical to understand the underlying reasons for BPD behaviors to rebuild relationships and keep everyone safe during a crisis. It's vital to educate yourself, your friends, and family members on BPD, as well as any other mental health difficulties you or a loved one with BPD may be experiencing.

- Spending time with someone you care about is a wonderful way to receive and provide support. Keeping the worried person occupied and amused while ensuring their safety.

- Simply by being in their presence, they are physically healthy. It may be difficult for someone with BPD to explain or even consider motivating them in a crisis. When the person with BPD is physically well, it is good to plan ahead of time for a catastrophe.

- BPD is a disorder that can be treated. While persons with BPD may have crises from time to time, you should learn how to assist yourself, or a loved one live a normal, comfortable, and secure existence.

People with BPD may easily lose confidence due to the "stigma associated" with the disorder and the incorrect idea that it is incurable, particularly when they slip into the dark spiral of sad emotions that commonly follow a crisis.

8.2 Helping Someone with BPD

What can you do if you have a family member or acquaintance who has been diagnosed with "BPD"? Even if you can't compel them to receive treatment, you should try to enhance contact, create appropriate limits, and maintain a strong relationship.

While an older female clinician attends to her, a young girl glances down at the "thumbs" of her clenched fists held together in front of her.

What should you know About BPD?

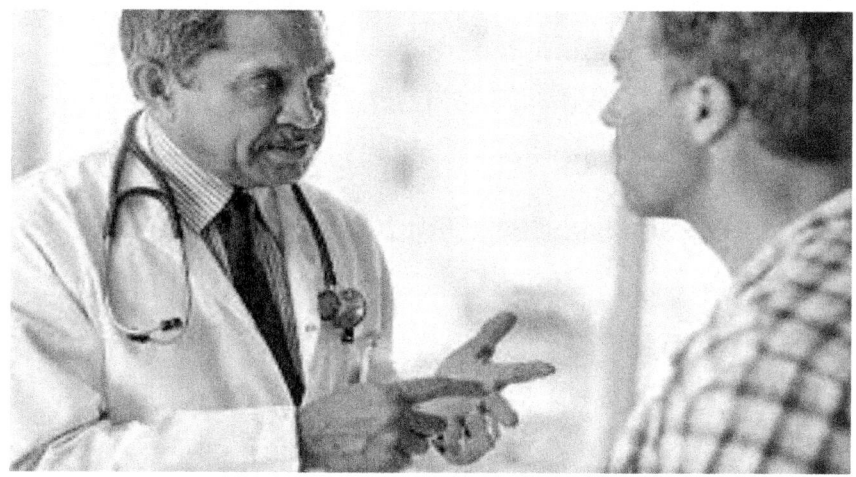

Individuals with BPD may find it challenging to form relationships, particularly with those closest to them. Because of their unexpected mood swings, angry outbursts, chronic abandonment anxieties, and impulsive & illogical actions, loved ones will feel powerless, battered, and out of sorts. Partners and family members often describe relationships with BPD persons as an intense "roller coaster" with no end in sight. You may feel helpless and imprisoned in the face of one of your loved one's BPD symptoms until you "end the connection"; otherwise, the individual receives therapy. On the other side, you are stronger than you believe.

Controlling your emotions, setting firm boundaries, and boosting communication with your loved one may all help you improve your bond. While there is no cure for BPD, with the correct therapy and support, many people with the condition may recover, and their "relationships" can become healthier and more meaningful. Patients with the most support and stability at home, on the other hand, recover more quickly than those with more tumultuous and insecure relationships.

Even if the person with "BPD" refuses to admit the issue or seek therapy, you will enhance both your relationship and your quality of life if your spouse, parent, infant, sibling, partner, or other loved one has BPD.

Learning all the things you can

It's vital to consider your loved one's suffering, whether or not they have BPD. Self-destructive and harmful acts are the result of deep emotional distress. To put it another way, they aren't for you. Understand that when a loved one hurts you, it is typically out of a wish to alleviate the suffering they are "experiencing," not out of malice. Learning about BPD won't make your relationship troubles disappear, but it will help you better recognize what you're doing and cope with challenges.

Recognizing the signs & symptoms of BPD

It's not always simple to spot the signs and symptoms of BPD. Other mental diseases, such as depression, bipolar disorder, anxiety, an "eating disorder," or drug misuse, are often diagnosed alongside BPD. Minor incidents might cause your "family member" or beloved one with BPD to have extreme emotions. Borderline people are unable to think rationally or rest comfortably when agitated. They can say hurtful things and behave in risky or improper ways. Family members, spouses, and friends may have conflicts due to their emotional instability.

Many people who have close contact with someone who has BPD are aware that something is wrong with them, but they have no idea what it is or whether it has a name. Finding out you have BPD maybe both be reassuring and hopeful.

8.3 Communication tips

It's critical to know when it's appropriate to initiate a discussion. Now is not the time to speak to your loved one if someone is furious, physically aggressive, or makes violent threats. It's preferable to gently postpone the subject by stating, "Let's speak tomorrow when you're both comfortable." You'd want to give you your complete attention right now, but it's too difficult for you."

When things are good (calmer):

Listen actively & be sympathetic.

Distractions such as the television, screen, or mobile phone may be avoided. It is not good to interrupt or shift the discussion to your interests. Set your choice aside, avoid assigning blame or criticism, and "nod" or make short vocal remarks like "yes" or "uh-huh" to indicate attention to what the other person is saying. To indicate that you're paying attention and sympathizing, you don't have to "agree" with what the other person is doing.

Focus on the "emotions," not the words.

People with BPD talk more successfully with their ideas than with their words. People with BPD need to have their pain validated and acknowledged. Instead of striving to "reconcile" the words stated, pay attention to any feelings your buddy is attempting to express.

Have an effort to make a person suffering from BPD feel noticed.

If they're acting irrationally, don't attempt to convince them that they're wrong, win the debate, or dismiss their feelings.

And if the individual with "BPD" is acting out, try to remain calm.

Avoid getting enraged when faced with allegations and critiques, no matter how unjust they seem. If you attempted to protect yourself, your partner would get outraged. If you need some time and space to relax, take a step back.

When feelings are high, try to divert your loved one's attention.

It will help if you can shift your loved one's focus away from you, but the most effective diversion is a calming hobby. Exercise, listen to music, drink hot tea, groom a horse, draw, gardening, or clean the home are all feasible options.

Discuss topics about something other than the disorder.

Make time to learn about and discuss other hobbies so that you and your loved one may live lives that aren't dictated by disease. De-stressing conversations on lighter topics may enable your partner to pursue new hobbies or rekindle existing ones.

Self-destructive habits & suicide threats should not be overlooked.

Do not forsake a loved one who seems to be on the verge of killing themselves. Make an appointment with your loved one's psychiatrist.

Setting healthy boundaries with a loved one having borderline.

Setting and enforcing appropriate limitations or restrictions is one of the most important ways to help a loved one with "BPD" maintain control over their behavior. Setting boundaries may help your loved one deal with the demands of the real world, where institutions like schools, businesses, and the legal system, for example, set and enforce strict limits on what is and isn't acceptable behavior.

You'll have more options for coping with disruptive behavior when you create boundaries in your relationship, replacing the vagueness and instability of your present scenario with a sense of order. You'll be able to establish a sense of trust and loyalty between you if both sides respect the limitations, which are crucial components in any successful relationship.

On the other hand, boundaries aren't a quick remedy for a broken relationship. Things can become a little worse before they get better. BPD patients are afraid of being rejected and are easily insulted. If you set limits in your "relationship" for the first time, your partner is likely to respond negatively. Giving in to your loved one's fury or hostility will only serve to encourage their bad behavior and perpetuate the cycle. Keeping your commitment and sticking to your decisions, on the other hand, will inspire you, benefit your spouse, and maybe change your relationship.

How to set & reinforce healthy boundaries

Talk about limitations with your husband while you're both calm and not in the middle of an argument. Make it clear what human behaviors you will and will not accept. "If you can't speak to him without yelling obscenities at him, He'll walk out," you may say to a loved one.

Do:

- Set boundaries with the individual with BPD in a calm way. "You love him and want your relationship to flourish, but you can't bear the stress generated by his behavior," you may say. "You're counting on him to make this adjustment for you." Ascertain that everyone in the house is aware of the rules and how to enforce them if they are violated.

- Instead of seeing constraints as a particular situation, think of them as a strategy. Rather than bombarding your spouse with a lengthy list of restrictions all at once, present them one or two at a time.

Don't:

- Make promises and set deadlines that you know you will not keep. Human nature demands that your loved one eventually push the boundaries you set. If you give in and don't follow through with the consequences, your loved one will know the ineffective barrier and will continue to misbehave. Ultimatums are only used in the most difficult situations (& again, you should be prepared to follow it through).

- Allow unregulated coercive conduct to continue. No one should be verbally or physically attacked. Because a personality disorder causes your loved one's behavior, it is no less genuine or harmful to you or other family members.

- Protect the person with BPD from the repercussions of their behavior to empower them. You may have to leave if your loved one refuses to respect your limits and tries to make you feel uncomfortable. It doesn't mean you don't care about them; nonetheless, you should prioritize your health.

Supporting your beloved, one's "BPD" treatment.

Even though BPD is extremely treatable, many individuals who suffer from it refuse to seek help or deny a problem. Even if this is a family member or friend, you should provide advice, increase interaction, and establish limits while encouraging them to get psychological assistance.

Though drug choices are limited, the advice of a trained therapist may help your loved one get back on track. DBT (Dialectical Behavior Therapy) and schema-focused therapy are two BPD treatments that will help the loved one with friendship and confidence concerns and learn new coping strategies. They will learn to slow down the hormonal storm and self-soothe in healthy ways in therapy.

How to support treatment

If your partner refuses to admit that they have "BPD," you may wish to try couple's counseling. This letter emphasizes friendship and greater communication rather than focusing on your loved one's illness. Your spouse will be more likely to commit and seek BPD treatment in the future if you do this.

To learn how to handle stress and emotions safely, encourage your loved one to try mindfulness and calming activities like meditation, deep breathing, or yoga. They may also use sensory-based signals to ease stress momentarily. You may engage in all of these treatments for your loved ones, strengthening your link and encouraging them to try new therapies. Your loved one will learn to hit stop when the need to act out or behave impulsively emerges due to their capacity to bear the discomfort. The "Emotional Intelligence Toolkit" from Help Guide is self-guided software that shows your loved one how to ride the "wild horse" of intense emotions while remaining calm and focused.

Setting goals for "BPD" recovery:

It is crucial. Be patient and set reasonable expectations while aiding a loved one in recovery. Change occurs, but it takes time, just as altering a habit pattern does. Take little steps instead of striving for enormous, unattainable objectives that will only result in failure and sorrow for you and your loved one. Setting modest, manageable objectives and lowering your expectations might help you and your loved one achieve more.

Supporting the healing of a loved one may be both difficult and gratifying. You must look for yourself; yet the process will aid you in growing as a person and enhancing your relationship.

8.4 How to Be a Better Friend to Someone having BPD

Connecting with a borderline personality disorder might be challenging (BPD). Your friend may feel lost or weak at times, leaving you feeling powerless as well. Although there is no cure for BPD, people with the disorder may recover with the correct therapy and support. Below are a few basic suggestions for becoming a close friend to someone with BPD.

Edify Yourself Regarding BPD

If you have a buddy who suffers from BPD, you should educate yourself on the disorder. Instability in feelings and sentiments characterizes the condition, which influences relationships and attitudes. As a result, friendships between people with BPD will be difficult. People who suffer from BPD are more likely to engage in manipulative, harsh, or disruptive conduct.

If you have a thorough understanding of the disease, you'll recognize these actions for what they are: symptoms. Understanding that these actions aren't meant to hurt you might help you empathize with your buddy and offer more compassion.

Encourage them to seek professional assistance.

It is seldom effective in persuading individuals to seek medical assistance, regardless of how urgently they want it (unless, of course, an emergency scenario exists). You can, however, encourage your friends to seek assistance if they so desire.

It might include telling your friend that you're "proud of them" for seeking treatment or that you believe seeking therapy is a terrific decision. It could entail providing transportation to meetings or making an effort to visit them in the hospital. Whatever you do, make sure your friend knows you're rooting for them. Those with BPDs who have care and stability in their personal lives find their symptoms improve more quickly than those who do not.

Validate Experiences of Your Friend.

The essential thing is to pay attention to and validate the sentiments of a buddy. You can help them feel better in whatever way you choose. Recognize that outbursts of emotion are a frequent indication of the condition. You may not agree with their assessment of the situation or believe their strong feelings are warranted, but you must listen to and understand their anguish.

Receiving support from another person will be useful for those suffering from BPD. Most people with "BPD" were reared in socially isolated circumstances and believed that no one cared about their thoughts or feelings. Because of the disorder's origins, even those who did not grow up in a difficult environment may have become used to being told they are exaggerating. Consequently, finding someone concerned about their well-being might be beneficial.

Don't Ignore the Threats of Harm

People with BPD often make suicide threats and gestures. Individuals with "BPD" often make suicide threats, causing family and friends to become "desensitized" to such conduct. Also, if your friend has made suicidal threats but has never tried or finished suicide, be aware that people with "BPD" are far more likely to try and accomplish suicide. According to studies, 75% of people with BPD will attempt suicide at some time throughout their lives. According to a study, between 3% and 10% of people with BPD commit suicide. As a result, never dismiss a suicide sign, even if you don't believe they'll go through with it.

Learn the warning signs of a friend considering suicide and contact 911 if you fear there is a danger that your friend may hurt themselves. Professionals should determine if there is a serious risk of injury.

Also, Take Care of Yourself.

Relationships with people who suffer from "BPD" may become unbalanced, and you may feel as if you're giving more than you're receiving. If this happens just once in a while, it's typically a good thing. There are ups and downs in most marriages; no relationship can be great all of the time. However, if you are always in an unbalanced and anxious state, your relationship will suffer.

According to research, friends and relatives who care for people with "BPD" had increased rates of aggression, anxiety, despair, and mistrust. Families often experience financial difficulty, marital troubles, and social disgrace. You may get angry or worried if you offer too much. You may feel compelled to quit a relationship for your enjoyment and well-being after some time.

Having a loyal, trustworthy friend, on the other hand, is more beneficial to persons with BPD in the long run than having a friend who was completely there for a few months before vanishing forever. As a result, it's critical that you look after yourself, take periodic breaks from your friend as required, and establish proper boundaries so that you may meet your own needs.

Speaking is more superior to doing. You'll need active listening skills and a high level of self-awareness to figure out when it's time to take a step back. If you put out the effort, you can have a long-term, meaningful relationship with someone who has BPD.

Conclusion

Those suffering from BPD may find it difficult to perform some high-level cognitive processes, such as mood management and self-control. While performing these activities, they draw on the collective intelligence of others in their immediate vicinity to complement their own. It is necessary to be near an external object or person to use them as part of one's cognitive equipment. It is also necessary to have a very deep informational connection with them. The anxiety and anguish experienced by BPD patients, especially in the face of abandonment, might be explained by the fact that desertion entails losing one's mind. Any effort or risk may feel essential to escape such a loss. The expanded mind idea is also used to treat a wide range of mental illnesses.

After reading this book, you should have understood that it covers almost every aspect of borderline personality disorder, which is a positive realization. From the introduction through the history of borderline personality disorder to the conclusion of BPD triggers, each of the 10 chapters provides a concise summary of borderline personality disorder.

Whether you or a loved one, friend or family member is suffering from BPD, this book will aid you in detecting and overcoming all of the issues that may be causing you concern.

Many topics will make your or someone else's life simpler and easier. These include symptoms of BPD, different types of BPD, diagnosis, treatment and management, BPD and suicide prevention, self-help, helping others, BPD in families, the recovery process, common misconceptions about BPD, and triggers. It will almost certainly improve your overall quality of life, including how you deal with everyday problems and how you connect with other people.

This book has a wealth of information that will certainly aid you in conquering your life's obstacles and avoiding melancholy, worry, tension, and fury from occurring.

Printed in Great Britain
by Amazon